Wesley and the Quadrilateral

Wesley and the Quadrilateral

RENEWING THE CONVERSATION

W. Stephen Gunter
Scott J. Jones
Ted A. Campbell
Rebekah L. Miles
Randy L. Maddox

Abingdon Press
Nashville

WESLEY AND THE QUADRILATERAL:
RENEWING THE CONVERSATION

Copyright © 1997 by Abingdon Press

All Rights Reserved.

Library of Congress Cataloging-in-Publication Data

Wesley and the quadrilateral: renewing the conversation / W. Stephen
    Gunter ... [et al.].
        p.   cm.
    Includes bibliographical references.
    ISBN 0-687-06055-9 (alk. paper)
    1. Wesley, John, 1703–1791—Contributions in Biblical interpretation.
    2. Bible–Criticism, interpretation, etc.–History.   3. United Methodist
    Church–Doctrines–History.   4. Methodist Church–Doctrines–History.
    I. Gunter, W. Stephen, 1947– .
    BX8495.W5W47   1997
    230'.7'01–dc21   97-19088
                                                                                    CIP

Unless otherwise noted, all Scripture quotations are from the New Revised Standard Version Bible, copyright © 1989 by the Division of Christian Education of the National Council of the Churches of Christ in the USA. Used by permission.

Scripture quotations noted as AV are from the King James Version of the Bible

Portions of chapter two have previously been published in Scott J. Jones, *John Wesley's Conception and Use of Scripture* (Nashville: Kingswood Books, 1995).

Portions of chapter three have previously been published in Ted A. Campbell, "Christian Tradition, John Wesley, and Evangelicalism," *Anglican Theological Review* 74/1 (Winter 1992): 54–67.

This book is printed on recycled, acid-free, elemental-chlorine–free paper.

97 98 99 00 01 02 03 04 05 06 — 10 9 8 7 6 5 4 3 2 1

Contents

Whether the Word Be Preached or Read
Charles Wesley, 1783 (2 Cor. 3:5-6)

Whether the Word be preached or read,
no saving benefit I gain
from empty sounds or letters dead;
unprofitable all and vain,
unless by faith thy word I hear
and see its heavenly character.

Unmixed with faith, the Scripture gives
no comfort, life, or light to see,
but me in darker darkness leaves,
implunged in deeper misery,
overwhelmed with nature's sorest ills.
The Spirit saves, the letter kills.

If God enlighten through his Word,
I shall my kind Enlightener bless;
but void and naked of my Lord,
what are all verbal promises?
Nothing to me, till faith divine
inspire, inspeak, and make them mine.

Jesus, the appropriating grace
'tis thine on sinners to bestow.
Open mine eyes to see thy face;
open my heart thyself to know.
And then I through thy Word obtain
sure present, and eternal gain.

From *The United Methodist Hymnal* (Nashville: The United Methodist Publishing House, 1989), #595.

Introduction

"Wesley believed that the living core of the Christian faith was revealed in Scripture, illumined by tradition, vivified in personal experience, and confirmed by reason." — *The Book of Discipline of The United Methodist Church, 1996*, ¶68, p. 74.

Perhaps no theological topic has been the focus of more debate within The United Methodist Church over the past quarter century than the "Wesleyan Quadrilateral," the popular name for the claims in the opening quotation. Such prominence, particularly given the initial novelty of the expression, has earned it the characterization of being a "modern Methodist myth."[1] This book might well be considered an exercise in demythologizing this myth. Understood in the typical modern sense of this term, we are concerned to distinguish the historical realities about Wesley and the Quadrilateral from fanciful "myths" that have made their way into recent debates. Understood in the more classic sense of the term, we hope to identify some of the foundational convictions that find illuminating expression in the "myth" of the Wesleyan Quadrilateral.

Some historical background will help to put this twofold goal in perspective. When the Evangelical United Brethren and The Methodist Church voted to merge as The United Methodist Church in 1968, one of the immediate needs created was the development of a doctrinal statement to succeed the respective E.U.B. Confession of Faith and Methodist Articles of Religion. The committee charged with this task initially considered creating a new integrative "creed" to articulate the doctrinal commitments of The United Methodist Church. It did not take long to realize the prolonged controversy that would attend such an effort, as competing forces lobbied over every potential alteration of the earlier standards. In the face of this prospect the committee was pushed toward a less ambitious option. The committee decided to retain both of the predecessor creeds, but to designate them as "landmark documents" and supplement them with a newly developed statement on the contemporary theological task of The United Methodist Church.[2] The core of this new supplementary statement (officially adopted in the 1972 *Book of Discipline of The United Methodist Church*) was the assertion that contemporary doctrinal reflection and construction in The United Methodist Church should be guided by four *interdependent* sources or guidelines: Scripture, tradition, experience, and reason.

Time has shown that what this compromise lacked in ambition it made up for in ambiguity. Three cases in point stand out. First is the ambiguity surrounding the nature of "doctrinal standards." The official title of the committee that developed this compromise was the Commission on Doctrine and Doctrinal Standards. Since the statement on the contemporary "Theological Task" was the focus of their creative work, one can see how the subject of this statement, the four sources or guidelines, might come to be called "doctrinal standards" in informal contexts. And this has indeed often happened, even though the actual statement adopted in the *Discipline* carefully confined this label to the landmark documents of the respective denominations with their doctrinal affirmations, while referring to Scripture, tradition, experience and reason instead as "doctrinal guidelines." The impact of the contrary informal practice has been a clouding in United Methodist circles (reflected as well in broader Methodist/Wesleyan circles) of the important distinction between (1) doctrinal convictions themselves and (2) the criteria for theological reflection. The result is a subtle but persistent tendency to mistakenly identify the affirmation of the four guidelines with the former category (doctrinal standards) rather than the latter (guidelines).

The second ambiguity in the compromise embodied in the 1972 *Discipline* statement can be found in the term "quadrilateral" as a name for the four guidelines of theological reflection. Actually, this term is never used in the official *Discipline* statement, but it was used in an interim report submitted in 1970, and it quickly became the unofficial label for the contemporary emphasis of the church, namely that United Methodist theological reflection should draw not only on Scripture and tradition, but reason and experience as well. The ambiguity here lies in the connotations of "quadrilateral." Is it simply an affirmation of the fourfold nature of criteria for theological reflection, or does it imply some type of equality among the four? In the years following 1972, there was growing concern in some circles that the theological primacy of Scripture was not appropriately affirmed in the popular image of the Quadrilateral or in the actual descriptions of the Theological Task statement in the *Discipline*. Related concerns were voiced on a smaller scale about the relative authority of tradition (including the "landmark documents") in United Methodist theology.

The third ambiguity in the 1972 compromise proved to be the question of the connection between Wesley and the emphasis on the four guidelines for contemporary theological reflection. Here again the 1972 *Discipline* statement was less forthright than the 1970 interim report. While the earlier report had cited Wesley as explicit warrant for the fourfold emphasis, the *Discipline* statement avoided mention of Wesley in the discussion of the four guidelines. This reticence reflected the fact that some were already raising historical questions about the connection: Could a conscious and consistent emphasis on the four guidelines really be demonstrated in Wesley? And, even if it was evident in Wesley, was it something *distinctive* of him? Questions like these continued to grow after 1972.

The initial idea for this book took shape in the midst of debates over the various ambiguities in the 1972 *Discipline* statement. Its roots go back at least a decade, when several of us were participants in the Wesley Studies Group at the 1987 meeting of the Oxford Institute of Methodist Theological Studies. As students of Wesley who were engaged in detailed research on various aspects of his theological method, we understood that some historically inaccurate notions of a Wesleyan Quadrilateral were involved on all sides of the debate, and these needed to be redressed. More important, we believed that the emerging emphasis on the fourfold guidelines in Methodist/ Wesleyan theological circles could benefit from a clearer sense of how Wesley himself understood and drew upon Scripture, tradition, reason, and experience.

This led us to contemplate producing a collection of essays that delineated with a high degree of historical and theological precision what John Wesley believed and taught about the components of the Quadrilateral. Other commitments kept the original participants from moving ahead with the project at that time, and within a couple of years the pressing need for the project appeared to subside. This was in part because Donald Thorsen had published *The Wesleyan Quadrilateral: Scripture, Tradition, Reason and Experience as a Model of Evangelical Theology*, which gathered evidence of Wesley's appeals to each of the four guidelines and stressed the primacy of Scripture among the four. Even more important was the adoption of a revised "Theological Task" statement in the 1988 *Book of Discipline of The United Methodist Church*. This revised statement anchored the four theological guidelines more solidly in Wesley's example, while avoiding excessive claims of either originality or distinctiveness on his part. It also made the primacy of Scripture among the guidelines more explicit than the 1972 *Discipline*. Finally, it tried to underline the distinction between doctrinal affirmations and theological exploration.[3]

Whatever the benefits of the 1988 revision, it has not proven to be a panacea that resolves all differences among United Methodists about theological method. Indeed, the debate over these issues has emerged with renewed vigor in the last couple of years. As before, this debate is being framed broadly in terms of perceived strengths or weaknesses of the notion of a Wesleyan (or Methodist) Quadrilateral. If there is a difference in the current debate, it is that it is focusing less on questions about historical precedents in Wesley than on disagreements about the contemporary philosophical and/or theological adequacy of the Quadrilateral. One pole of this present debate is ably represented by John B. Cobb, Jr., in his volume *Grace and Responsibility*.[4] As one very sensitive to the critique of many traditional Christian beliefs and practices raised by contemporary groups and concerns, Cobb is drawn to the connotations of the Quadrilateral that emphasize the full integrity of (contemporary) experience and reason alongside (past) Scripture and tradition. At times he expresses this in terms of a "dialectical" relationship where each is subject to criticism, correction, and supplementation by the others. But at other times he seems to cast the four elements in some opposition with each other, emphasizing primarily the prerogative of "relatively autonomous reason and experience" to stand in judgment of Scripture and tradition. In all of this his stated intention is clear, "I have found that most of those who call for a renewal of the study of Wesley do not suppose that Wesley's thought can be simply repeated today. Instead, they rightly believe that the movement he initiated needs to reappraise his work and the relevance of his thought for our time in order to find a shared basis on which to move forward. . . . The time for such efforts has come."

The sharpest response to such emphases in Cobb and others has been issued by William J. Abraham in *Waking from Doctrinal Amnesia*.[5] Interestingly, Abraham concedes to Cobb that while the stated goal of the Quadrilateral may have been to stress the interdependence of

Scripture, tradition, reason, and experience in theological reflection, the inevitable result of such language in the modern arena has been that reason and experience win out over Scripture and tradition. This leads Abraham to argue that United Methodists should scrap the Quadrilateral as "a hastily contrived shotgun wedding between scripture and tradition . . . and reason and experience." He bases this argument in part on the ease with which the stated purpose of the Quadrilateral is set aside, construing it instead as a methodology by which, "If you cannot get what you desire on one ground, pass laterally to the next until you do." His deepest concern, however, is a conviction that the emphasis on the Quadrilateral continues to foster confusion between doctrinal standards and the criteria of theological reflection. He laments the tendency of United Methodists to look for their identity in the way in which they "do" theology, rather than in what they actually believe doctrinally. The end result is, "We have become so doctrinally indifferent and illiterate that the church is starved of intellectual content."

The renewed ferment around our topic, expressed in the contrast between Cobb and Abraham, rekindled the interest of the participants in that original conversation at Oxford regarding a book on the Quadrilateral. This time we drew into our conversation a couple of new contributors with professional training in contemporary theology, who combined this training with an interest in Wesley Studies. Our initial overtures convinced us that we shared some common concerns about the typical structure and polarization of the present debate. On the one hand, we were unconvinced by those who claimed that the very notion of the Quadrilateral was inherently wrongheaded or unWesleyan. On the other hand, we found some of the strongest defenders of the Quadrilateral to be championing conceptions of the nature of Scripture, tradition, reason, and experience (as well as the interplay among them) that are in our judgment both ill fitting to Wesley and (just as important) inadequate to the challenges facing the church today. As our conversations continued, we became intrigued by the possibility that a fresh reconsideration of Wesley's own conception and use of Scripture, tradition, reason, and experience might offer one of the most relevant and helpful contributions to the present debate.

This left us facing the question of how such a reconsideration might best be pursued. One immediate point of agreement among us was that the present discussions seem to be characterized too much by *debate* in which recalcitrant opponents compete in the interest of winning. The obvious alternative was authentic *dialogue*, which aims at building mutual understanding and (ideally) consensus. Put in classic Methodist terms, this was the alternative of holding "conference" about the issues of theological method. We recognized that our initial conversations were budding attempts at such conference, and we have committed ourselves to carrying this process to a deeper level over the past year. In all frankness, our experience proved as valuable in reminding us of the demands of real "conference" as it did it in letting us sample the benefits of this "means of grace" (as Wesley always insisted it to be). The realities of teaching schedules, family life, and publication deadlines gradually undercut our original ideal of a truly joint-authored work sharing the consensus of our "subset" of the larger Methodist conference. The ideal surrendered, we remained convinced that we had something worth contributing to the larger ongoing conversation. We each have found our own convictions and perspectives on particular aspects of the larger debate informed, refined, and enriched by the level of conference that we have been able to enjoy. While we have some remaining differences, we decided to offer the fruits of our conference to the larger Methodist community (and other interested parties) in hopes of converting more of the present debate into dialogue.

In practice, this meant that each of us took primary responsibility for one chapter in the book. The assignments were as follows: Stephen Gunter, "The Quadrilateral and the 'Middle Way'"; Scott Jones, "The Rule of Scripture"; Ted Campbell, "The Interpretive Role of Tradition"; Rebekah Miles, "The Instrumental Role of Reason"; Randy Maddox, "The Enriching Role of Experience." Each of us drafted our chapter and circulated it among the others, drawing on their responses and suggestions for revision (though not shying away from suggesting areas of remaining difference). The Introduction and Conclusion are more jointly authored, with Stephen taking on the responsibility for the initial and final drafts, just as he was primarily responsible for gathering us together, trying to keep us on task, and editing the entirety of the volume.

Finally, a word on style. We have not tried to write a book for the theological academy, although all the authors are active in their respective academic guilds. This book is an exercise in "ecclesial theology"—theology by the church and for the church. It is written by people who are, or have been, involved as pastors, missionaries, and teachers of future pastors, missionaries, and teachers. As persons who are deeply involved in The United Methodist Church at the parish, conference, and General Conference levels, we have written for those in our own denomination and beyond in the Wesleyan tradition who are involved as pastors, bishops, seminary teachers, seminary students, administrators, and laity. We have written in order to address a specific theological, but very practical, issue—the meaning, interpretation, and use of the Quadrilateral by United Methodists today. We offer our readers the results of our own "conferencing" on Wesley and the Quadrilateral, in the hope of enriching and renewing the conversation about this vital issue.

Chapter One

The Quadrilateral and the "Middle Way"

W. Stephen Gunter

It is well known that John Wesley was an Anglican priest, and remained so all his life, yet the theological implications of this historic Anglican identity are not widely recognized. Although it is difficult to isolate and define *exactly* what these theological implications are, some key Anglican personalities prior to Wesley outline a distinctive theological frame of reference. And while many Methodists assume that the contours of this perspective originated with John Wesley (or perhaps in recent decades with Albert Outler and the "Wesleyan Quadrilateral"), they actually emerged two centuries prior to Wesley. The practical implication of this is that when we use the Quadrilateral—especially Scripture, tradition, and reason—we are *potentially* in continuity with a stream of theological identity much older than Methodism itself. To gain some perspective on what this means, it is important to clarify the significance of John Wesley's Anglicanism. Unless the implications of this are understood in at least a summary fashion, the following historical discussion may seem irrelevant to the theological issue at hand.

As an Anglican, Wesley viewed the authority of Scripture from a perspective significantly different from that of the non-Anglican evangelicals of the eighteenth century, especially the Dissenters, the eighteenth-century descendants of the Puritans. Both agreed that Scripture is authoritative, but we will see that the particulars of this authority were not the same. At the risk of oversimplification, one might say that the Dissenters, like their Puritan forebears, insisted that Scripture is *the* authority for *everything*, whereas the Anglican evangelicals emphasized its authority for issues related specifically to salvific knowledge. Scripture is authoritative primarily to relate to us *all* that we need to know for our salvation.

When we turn to tradition, the perspective of the Anglican

evangelical is even more in contrast to the Puritan tradition. Whereas the Anglicans highly esteemed the entirety of the Christian tradition, and in Wesley's day especially the first five centuries, the Puritan tradition displayed a distinct preference for the contours of Christian identity prevalent since the Reformation. And in this stream, the theological premises of Calvin stand out over those of Luther. Ultimately the Calvinist perspective inherent in the Puritan tradition left a permanent mark on Anglican theology, but in Wesley's day there was ample space to be staunchly Anglican without being staunchly Calvinist. Wesley occupied this space, and because of that he theologized quite differently from those of Puritan heritage. We are really talking about two significantly different streams of historic religious and theological consciousness.

In the process of describing the evolution and emergence of these theological working principles, we will encounter some very familiar names—royal figures like King Henry VIII, Queen Mary, and Queen Elizabeth I, as well as Cardinals, Archbishops, and Bishops, such as Wolsey, Cranmer, Parker, Jewel, Hooker, Tillotson, Andrewes, and Taylor. In contemporary society one can hardly imagine that Queen Elizabeth II or Prince Charles could have much theological impact on the Archbishop of Canterbury, but as we shall see, the late medieval world was quite a different place from ours. Royalty was quite influential, at times even determinative, in defining the theological emphases of Anglicanism.

The English Monarchy and the "Middle Way"

It is quite common to use the expression *via media* ("middle way")[1] to describe the path of Anglican theology, and the question that this implies is, "Middle way between what two alternatives?" There is some historical warrant for posing the question in this manner, for it is true that Anglican theological identity was forged between the opposing sides of traditional Roman Catholicism and Puritanism or Reformed Protestantism. Since the fundamental shaping of Anglican identity took place under Queen Elizabeth I, it is often referred to as the "Elizabethan Settlement." We must look first at why a "settlement" was necessary before turning our attention to how it took place. We also must reconsider the widely prevailing assumption that Queen Elizabeth I was a woman of little or no serious religious sentiment.[2]

18

The English intrigue began with the ultimately successful endeavors of Henry VIII (1509–1547) to divorce his wife, Catherine of Aragon, who previously had been the wife of Henry's elder brother, Arthur, who died in 1502.[3] Catherine had borne Henry no less than five children, all of whom died in infancy with the exception of one daughter, Mary. When Catherine had turned forty it became increasingly apparent that she would not produce a male heir, and besides, Henry had fallen in love with Anne Boleyn. In the Roman Catholic Church, divorce and remarriage required a papal dispensation declaring the previous marriage null and void. After five children and a life of fidelity on the part of Catherine, such a dispensation was not forthcoming despite the intercession of the former Archbishop of York, Cardinal Thomas Wolsey. The Pope had granted Henry the title "Defender of the Faith" (which the English sovereign still bears) because of his anti-Lutheran position on the Sacraments, but the only thing that was "null and void" on the issue of Henry's marriage was the chance that the Pope would grant a divorce from Catherine. While there were some noble precedents for the annulment of a royal marriage, it was politically an impossible move for Pope Clement VII, for Catherine was the aunt of the Holy Roman Emperor Charles V.

By 1531 Henry was becoming desperate. The year before he had forced Cardinal Wolsey out under an indictment of *Praemunire*, taking orders from a foreign power (the Pope and ostensibly Emperor Charles V). After replacing Wolsey with Thomas Cromwell, Henry still had to deal with the remainder of the clerical hierarchy. The king charged all of them *en masse* of a breach of *Praemunire* for having accepted Wolsey as legate, and then allowed each to rescue himself on two conditions—one, payment of a £100,000 fine; the other, acknowledgment of Henry as "Protector and only Supreme Head of the Church of England." It is significant that the £100,000 fine was not a major obstacle to the Bishops and Archbishops, but insulting the Pope and actually implicitly "breaking away from" Rome" were quite different matters. In the end the clergy compromised and acknowledged Henry as "Singular Protector, only and supreme Lord, and, as far as the law of Christ allows, even Supreme Head" of the Church in England. Henry had thus made the clergy admit responsibility for a crime they had not committed, and he persuaded them to accept the Crown as an essential part of the constitution of the English Church. Being now sovereign on all fronts, he could turn his full energies to the issue of divorce.

Henry ultimately divorced Catherine and married Anne Boleyn, who bore him a daughter, Princess Elizabeth. When Queen Anne failed to produce a male heir, Henry saw to her demise and married Catherine Parr, who bore King Henry the male heir that he coveted. Edward VI took the throne a pale and sickly child of nine, controlled, of course, by the reform-minded opportunists who surrounded him. On almost every front Henry had his way, but in reality the English Church was liturgically and theologically very much the same as in the decades prior to all his machinations. He had, however, set the stage for change; and his selected clerical leaders as well as his progeny would play the decisive roles in the liturgical and theological evolution of Anglican identity. One king and three wives, each bearing a child who would become sovereign over England. Add this familial complexity to the transitions between historic ecclesiastical identities, and you have a most interesting beginning to what came to be known as the "middle way."

At the death of Henry VIII in 1547, the churches of England looked much as they had always looked, and the services that were conducted in them were the services that parishoners experienced in virtually any other church in western Christendom, then or during the previous five hundred years, save the emerging radical Reformation groups. Liturgical reform, however, was in the air. Fourteen years earlier, in 1533, Henry had named the loyal and accommodating Thomas Cranmer as Archbishop of Canterbury. Unknown to Henry was Cranmer's sympathy toward Reformed theology and liturgical reform—which became abundantly clear after Henry's demise. Cranmer's greatest contribution was as the framer of successive editions of the Book of Common Prayer.

Even during the life of the king, Cranmer had been working on several innovations that spread widely in the space created by the death of Henry and the succession to the throne of the boy-king, Edward VI. The old church service had become so complicated, and the rules as what to read and when to recite so convoluted that, in Cranmer's own words, "Many times there was more business to find out what should be read, than to read it when it was found out." [4] There was a widely perceived need for greater simplicity. A second need was for more congregational participation in worship. In the later Middle Ages the laity had increasingly been placed in the position of spectators to ceremony rather than participants in celebrating the Christian faith. This gave rise to a third need, a liturgy in

20

the language of the people. One could hardly participate intelligently if the language were foreign. The fourth need was for the restoration of primitive customs such as the administration of the Holy Communion to the laity in both kinds, rather than bread only. Finally, there was need for greater edification through didactic sermons and regular reading of the Scriptures, both in the vernacular.[5] The call for these innovations became increasingly clear in successive editions of the Book of Common Prayer (1549, 1552, 1553). In 1552 Cranmer drew up the series of theological affirmations that ultimately become the Thirty-nine Articles in 1571, and are still retained in the Book of Common Prayer. These affirmations of the historic catholic faith (albeit with a discernible Calvinistic tint) were intended to give a doctrinal "platform" to the English Church, and they have since served to define the theological parameters that characterize the *via media*.[6]

The theological affirmations of the Thirty-nine Articles were viewed as declarations of theological unity with historic catholic (universal) Christianity, and formal subscription to them by clergy was required until the late nineteenth century. This most promising beginning at defining the theological identity of the English Church was accompanied by a similar attempt to define the legal status of the Church through a reform of Church Law, but this ran aground. And, indeed, all further reform was brought to an abrupt end by the death of the young King Edward on July 6, 1553, at the age of fifteen. Under Henry VIII the "formation" of the English Church had begun, and during the reign of his only son the "reformation" of the English Church took its first steps.

Due to the principle of male preference in inheritance, the youngest of Henry's three children was first to follow him on the throne. Because Edward was a minor and unable to rule in his own right, reform had taken quick root at the hands of his adult counselors. Edward was in turn succeeded by Henry's oldest daughter, Mary, the offspring of Catherine of Aragon. If ever there were a person constitutionally equipped to reverse a trend, it was surely Queen Mary. She was thirty-seven when she ascended, and she had lived all her adult life in virtual seclusion, since she and her mother had been driven out of the palace, objects both of scorn and of pity. It is no wonder that the traditional portrait of Mary is of a tight-lipped woman, stern, severe, and determined. And what Mary was determined to do was to turn back the clock to the way things were in her childhood—hence a return to Roman Catholicism. The five years of her reign (1553–58) are not of direct theological consequence for our purposes, but the events that took place under Mary's direction greatly colored the public mindset when she was succeeded by her half-sister, Elizabeth.

Mary was not only half-Spanish, she was also a devoted Roman Catholic. The political and ecclesial London "power brokers" who had led King Edward VI were fearful of her succession to the throne, but they were thwarted in an attempt to have Lady Grey proclaimed Queen. When Mary entered London as the rightful heir, the popular sentiment was that justice had prevailed, and she was met with tears of joy and songs of celebration. The English people had experienced only a few years of reform, prayer-books, and churches denuded of relics and shrines. The laity of the sixteenth century were even less interested than today's congregations in the technicalities of liturgy and theology, quite content to return things to the way they used to be.

Given the conservative and preserving nature of people, Mary might possibly have succeeded in restoring the English Church to the Roman Catholic fold, but there were two areas in which she seriously miscalculated. One was within her control and the other completely beyond her control. She could do nothing about the emotional depth and intensity with which some of the clerical leadership held the tenets of reform, and this alone would probably not have been insurmountable. It was the combination of this devotion and a decision of the monarch's own choosing that proved to be the Queen's fatal *faux pas*.

On January 12, 1554, there was signed at Westminster a marriage treaty for Mary that reflected both her partial Spanish descent and her unreserved commitment to Roman Catholicism—her matrimonial pledge to a Spanish kinsman, Prince Philip of Spain. As soon as this became known, England was caught in the throes of great alarm. The constant fighting in the Mediterranean political arena was of little consequence and no particular interest to the island nation, and the English were even less interested in becoming a tool of the Spanish. But Mary was monarch, and like her father, she never wavered once her intentions were announced. The marriage took place as planned on July 25, 1554, and as expected, steps were immediately forthcoming to pave the way for a return to the Roman fold.

The Roman reconciliation took place by means of two Parliamentary acts.[7] The first act reinstated the old laws against heresy and so made resistance to Mary's policies far more costly. The second act annulled all ecclesiastical legislation since 1528, with one exception—the dissolution of the monasteries. But even in the sixteenth century the British were showing a pragmatic and utilitarian streak, for they struck a compromise with the Pope. Parliament agreed to retract all the ecclesiastical legislation for the past thirty years if Rome would agree not to attempt to recapture the property of its members, wealth largely attained from the confiscation of the lands and furnishings of the churches and monasteries. This agreement was a blatant preservation of self-interest on the part of the members of Parliament.

This brief excursion into the intrigues of the reign of Queen Mary provides a context for discussing the key personalities that had shaped the emerging English theological identity. Queen Mary's decisions had placed the most prominent theological leadership in a most precarious position, and the stage was set for persecution and disaster. Since 1554 Archbishop Cranmer and Bishops Hugh Latimer and Nicholas Ridley had all been prisoners at Oxford. Latimer, a participant (during the reign of the boy-king Edward) in a movement designed to discourage superstition and promote sound learning, was a co-author along with Cranmer and others of the Homilies, a series of twelve didactic sermons on the Scriptures, justification, faith, and good works. When Latimer was executed on October 16, 1555, the English Church was deprived of a leader who was committed to the proposition that scriptural instruction through the medium of preaching was vital for the Church. Executed on the same day was Ridley, a courageous champion of Protestant principles who took special delight in destroying relics, which he viewed as symbols of superstition and channels of darkness.

Both Latimer and Ridley had been tried and condemned in summary fashion, but the more famous Cranmer could not be dealt with as expeditiously. Queen Mary had paid little or no attention to the executions of the lesser lights, but she really did not want to see Cranmer burn. She knew, as well, that it would be a monumental achievement were she to succeed in persuading Cranmer to recant. And, indeed, Cranmer did very nearly submit and stand by formal retractions.[8] He initially wrote out statements that retracted a few of his more distinctively Protestant positions. In his final confessions, however, Cranmer admitted that he had penned these out of fear and in a vain attempt to preserve life. Cranmer was a person of too

23

much integrity to recant just to save his own skin, and the sets of issues were too complex to solve simply by recanting propositions.

It was an unwilling Cranmer who had accepted the primacy of Canterbury in 1533 from Henry VIII, for Cranmer was primarily a scholar and theologian and only secondarily a politician. During the reigns of Henry and Edward, it was quite natural for him to support the changes that were taking place. He accepted the demand for loyalty to the king, and the ecclesial and theological changes effected during their respective reigns were of one accord with Cranmer's own conscience. With Queen Mary the issue of loyalty to the monarch was problematic in the extreme because her ecclesial, theological, and political convictions violated Cranmer's. At the age of sixty-five, his life's work clearly completed, the venerable old man was forced to make a most difficult choice—between a comfortable old age, and a ghastly and painful death by burning. The dictates of conscience were for Cranmer more powerful than the instincts of physical survival. On the day of his death at the burning stake at Smithfield, Cranmer plunged the hand that had signed his recantations into the flames, and according to tradition cried out: "This hand hath offended."

From every point of view Mary's reign was a failure. She had come to the throne with a sense of vocation and had tried to do what she believed was providential and right. She failed, not for lack of conviction, but for lack of timing. Too many people had gone too far in doctrinal and ecclesial matters to change their minds. Reforming theological principles and experience-directed liturgical practices had taken root too deeply in the minds of too many, and the veracity of these principles was only reinforced by the testimonial martyrdom of those who faced the fires of Smithfield rather than recant. Mary's death on November 17, 1558, followed within a few hours by the death of the Archbishop Reginald Pole, who had replaced Cranmer at Canterbury, seemed to many like a providential deliverance.

When Henry's daughter by Anne Boleyn ascended to the throne, the legitimacy of her crown rested on the legitimacy of her father's divorce from Catherine of Aragon and his subsequent marriage to her mother. The question was thus not *whether* Protestant reform would continue, but *how* Queen Elizabeth would continue reform without further traumatizing the English people. Was she a woman of political intrigue and duplicity, like her father and sister before her, or was she cut from a different bolt of cloth?

The Theologians and the "Middle Way"

Although we have been able to sketch in only the boldest contours the events and decisions that set the English reformation in motion, it is important to underscore what seem to be the most pertinent theological points that undergirded these events. Foremost is the work of Cranmer in formulating the original Book of Common Prayer, and along with others in the development of the Homilies. It would fall to others to spell out in more detail all the implications of these, but even before Elizabeth ascended to the throne, the points about scriptural instruction, liturgy that can be experienced and comprehended (especially scriptural sermons) by the general population, the affirmation of historic theological doctrines, all for the end of dispelling darkness and superstition and keeping the English Church in continuity with the primitive apostolic church, these and more were sufficiently clear for all to see. There were, however, several issues of Parliament that had to be settled before the "Elizabethan Settlement" could proceed. Few people put much trust in this slim young woman of barely twenty-five, but expectant eyes naturally turned her way when she took the throne in 1558.

England was divided ecclesiastically into three groups. There were those of Roman Catholic inclination who had supported Queen Mary, and who, of course, were still in positions of power and influence. Their followers among the parochial clergy were legion, but many of these were loyal to their local Bishop, whether he be Protestant or Catholic. On the other side were a very large number of clergy that had been deprived of their living and forced to live in seclusion. They were ready to be joined by a host of Protestant-minded clerics who had fled England, but now made ready to return should the new queen prove to be inclined toward Reformation principles. And between these two was a "middle group," who wished to have neither servility to Rome (the Pope) nor subservience to Geneva (John Calvin), but rather a Church of England truly "catholic" in all essentials and yet rid of the superstition and abuses that had gathered around it during the Middle Ages.

Elizabeth's first Parliament met in January 1559 and passed two acts of prime importance—the *Act of Supremacy* and the *Act of Uniformity*, which together form the judicial foundation for what is known as the "Elizabethan Settlement." Ecclesially the Settlement centered on the Book of Common Prayer, the new Homilies, and the

Articles of Religion. The Act of Supremacy revived Henry's legislation against Rome and also Edward's act to restore the administration of the sacrament to the laity in both kinds. Among other significant declarations that reflected Elizabeth's sentiments, the language from the Henrican era about the monarch being "supreme head" was changed to "supreme governor of both Church and State."[9] The passage by Parliament of the Act of Uniformity may have been due more to pressure from certain Protestant quarters in London than to Elizabeth's express wishes; it reintroduced, with severe penalties for disobedience, what was for all practical purposes the Book of Common Prayer of 1552.[10] It was followed almost immediately by a set of Royal Injunctions,[11] which were very similar to the Edwardian Injunctions, but significantly with added admonitions to regular preaching and catechizing—a return to the Homilies and the theological affirmations of Cranmer's era.

Historians have most often viewed the Elizabethan Settlement and Elizabeth herself as being politically motivated, and have therefore seen the legislation enacted largely as compromising and characterized by expediency. While there can be little doubt that the desire for political, social, and ecclesial calm was a high priority, there is good reason to believe that Queen Elizabeth was motivated deeply by spiritual and theological conviction. This insight into her convictions is perhaps best reflected by her selection of Matthew Parker as Archbishop of Canterbury. Parker, who accepted his election with great reluctance, was consecrated by four Bishops—Barlow, formerly of Bath and Wells; Coverdale; Scory of Chicester; and Hodgkins, Suffragan Bishop of Bedford—all of whom had survived from earlier days. Thus the apostolic succession was preserved, and by the new primate other Bishops of like mind were consecrated and the vacant sees filled.

With Parker in place at Canterbury, it soon became evident that Elizabeth's "settlement" was more than a rickety compromise cobbled together holding the Catholic-minded and the Puritan-minded at bay. The theological idea that drove Elizabeth and Parker was the concept of comprehensiveness, and this was clearly marked with positive doctrinal direction. Both saw "their Church" securely anchored doctrinally in Scripture and the ancient authorities, and they asserted unbroken continuity between the Early Church and the Church of England. Parker wrote in 1564 to Sir William Cecil (framer of the Royal Injunctions mentioned above) about a conversation with the French Ambassador and the Bishop of Coutances that "in fine they professed that . . . we were in religion very nigh to them. I answered that . . . I would wish them to come nigher to us, *grounding ourselves (as we do) upon the Apostolic doctrine and pure time of the Primitive Church.*"[12] Under Parker's leadership the conviction grew that the Anglican Church was the recapturing of the Catholic faith of the Church when it was, as Bishop Lancelot Andrewes often put it, "at the best."

We are prone to accept that the Archbishop of Canterbury was driven by spiritual and theological precept, but what about the Queen? It is broadly assumed that Elizabeth sat lightly to religion and had as her supreme goal the preservation of peace and order in her kingdom. More careful and astute historical research cautions us against accepting the notion that the Queen was a purely political animal, a diplomat whose attitude to Church and faith was one of cool and detached calculation. Is it possible that there were deeply felt religious inclinations that supported her political wisdom in the selection of Elizabeth's Bishops and Archbishop?

Elizabeth's prayers and devotional poetry, written in French, Italian (her favorite language), and Greek, as well as in English, reveal a humble seeker for grace, deeply aware of the great responsibility she exercised on behalf of others. Time and again the reader encounters prayers for the Church—"Thy Church, My Care." The Queen repeatedly petitions God that she should be given grace to "nourish the Church" in order that "I may look only on the things which are to the praise of thy name and advantage of thy Church." One reads these accounts and knows that hers is a religion of the heart as well as the mind. While political ends were obviously present, to interpret the period known as the Elizabethan Settlement as a series of decisions and Parliamentary acts based on political expediency is inadequate if not quite wrongheaded.[13]

Recognizing the spiritual and theological motivation of Elizabeth and her Archbishop does not, however, mean that the difficulties they faced in establishing the English Church were easily solved by them. It is not an oversimplification to say that the Queen and Parker found lively political and religious opposition from two sides—the Roman Catholic and the Puritan. The Roman Catholic threat was both theological and political, with the political issue taking front seat early on. In 1568 Pope Pius V found a useful collaboration in Mary Queen of Scots (not to be confused with Queen Mary, the first daughter of Henry VIII).

Mary entered England in that year and with great effort rallied the Romanists in the northern part of the country to her side. In the minds of some, Mary's claim to the throne was a good deal better than Elizabeth's. Elizabeth was the daughter of Anne Boleyn, whose marriage with Henry VIII had never been recognized by the Church of Rome, while Mary was directly descended from Henry VII through his daughter Margaret, who had married James IV of Scotland. Not only did many regard the Queen of Scots as rightful heir to the English throne, Mary herself made it the ambition of her life to be recognized as such. In November, 1569, she was aided in this ambition by the Earls of Westmoreland and Northumberland, who raised a rebellion in the north, the purpose of which was to depose Elizabeth, place Mary on the throne, and restore the "true catholic religion" in England.

The rebels entered Durham Cathedral and held a Roman Mass, treading the English Prayer Book under foot. In spite of help from Rome, the Northern Rebellion was quickly and viciously suppressed. Rome's interpretation of this failure, however, was to believe that there was widespread hostility toward Elizabeth and distrust of the direction that she and Parker were taking England. A formal "trial" of Elizabeth *in absentia* followed at Rome. She was found guilty, excommunicated, and deposed, and all her subjects were dispensed from their oath of allegiance to her. The verdict was then embodied in a papal bull, *Regnans in excelsis*,[14] a copy of which was smuggled into England and nailed to the door of the Bishop of London's palace.

To those who wished to remain loyal to Rome, the papal bull was a disaster of the first magnitude. They had previously been allowed to live quietly and practice their faith, only being required to pay a small tax for the privilege of not having to worship in the parish churches. Suddenly and without warning, literally overnight, they were placed in the position of having to make a choice between the Pope of Rome and the Queen of England. For the papal bull left no room for equivocation: "We do command and charge all and every nobleman, subjects and people, and others aforesaid, that they presume not to obey her or her orders, mandates, and laws." The choice was between excommunication and death.

The papal bull of 1570 marks the final separation of England from Rome, and this separation made it incumbent on the English Church to define itself formally over against Rome. This first step of theological definition fell on the shoulders of Bishop John Jewel, but before we look at the specific theological distinctions, we must describe the opposition that Elizabeth faced from the other side—her struggle with the Puritans.

The Anglican-Puritan Dispute over Scripture

From the foregoing it is clear that the Romanists wished to *overthrow* the Church of England and restore the papal authority, but the Puritans were of a completely different mind. The Puritan intention was to *transform* the emerging English Church into what they believed the Church ought to be. There was nothing peculiarly political about their activities, and although many of the Puritan leaders remained in close communication with Calvin's Geneva (where many had fled during the Marian exile), there never was a question about their being directed by a foreign power, nor did the Puritans show any hostility toward the Queen herself. Following Thomas Cartwright's lead, their opposition to the Queen was entirely on spiritual and theological grounds, so they could not be tried or imprisoned on political charges. Moreover, there was nothing to keep Puritan leaders from holding important positions of power and responsibility in government or in the Anglican Church. The Puritan opposition to the Elizabethan Settlement can be expressed quite succinctly: The Book of Common Prayer smelled of Popery, "an imperfect book, culled and picked out of the popish dunghill."[15]

The Puritans were convinced that the Anglican Church was tainted with Romanism, and even more fundamentally "untrue to Scripture." The driving force behind the Puritan opposition was the influence of Geneva and the full Calvinist system that John Knox was already introducing into Scotland. This would mean the abolition of the episcopacy and the substitution of presbyteral government by assemblies and church-sessions, worship more in accordance with the liturgical practices of the Reformation churches, increases in the prerogatives of lay leadership, the prohibition of elaborate vestments, the ring in marriage, other ornaments and ceremonies. In other words, for all practical purposes the Puritans called for the dissolution liturgically (and to a certain extent theologically) of the Anglican Church. And their fundamental basis for expecting such sweeping and fundamental changes was the authority of Scripture. The Anglican system was not scriptural; the Puritan scheme was.

Salvation and the Central Authority of Scripture

The responsibility of answering the Puritans would fall eventually on Richard Hooker, a pupil of John Jewel, who had accepted the first charge from Archbishop Parker to distinguish the identity of the English Church from the Roman Catholic Church. So teacher and later pupil took up their pen to defend and define the theological distinctions of the Anglican identity, a "middle way" between Roman Catholicism and Puritan Protestantism. The theological distinctives that began to emerge during the reigns of Henry VIII and Edward VI are not lost from view but rather are carefully remembered and made foundational: foremost are theological affirmations in harmony with the primitive apostolic church, the priority of the Christian Scriptures to define those doctrines, and the primacy of preaching to make both of these live in the hearts and minds of the laity.

When Bishop Jewel accepted the primary responsibility for distinguishing the emerging Anglican Church from the church in Rome, his main emphasis was on the "primacy of God's Word in Scripture" as the basic criterion for doctrine and life. The two testaments were "the heavenly voices whereby God hath opened unto us his will," and they alone, containing all that was necessary for salvation, can quiet the restless heart of humanity. Closely connected to this soteriological center of scriptural authority is the conviction that "all the canonical Scriptures [are the] foundation . . . whereupon is built the church of God . . . the very sure and infallible rule whereby may be tried whether the church doth stagger and err and whereunto all ecclesiastical doctrines ought to be called to account."[16] Consonant with the earlier emphases of Thomas Cranmer, this is not an arid authoritarianism, but an echo of Scriptures' supreme call to singleness of heart and godliness of life. In the Preface to the *Great Bible* published in 1539, Cranmer had written regarding the Christian Scriptures: "the most preciouse Juell and most holy relyque that remayneth upon earth."[17] It is as "necessary for the lyfe of man's soule, as for the body to breath."[18] The point of this for Cranmer is not that people should master the Bible, but that God through the Bible will master people. Cranmer's conclusion is that a person should bring to the study of Scripture the fear of God, "and then next a fyrme and stable purpose to refourme his owne selfe," and furthermore to live an exemplary life, "whych is sure the moost lyvele and effecteous fourme and maner of teachynge."[19]

When Archbishop Parker selected Bishop Jewel as the one most able to develop an apologetic for Anglicanism, he knew well the one he had chosen, and he recognized the importance of the greatest possible harmony between what one Bishop was writing and what other famous reform-minded Bishops had preached. Latimer, who had resigned his see as a matter of principle toward the end of Henry's reign, was the greatest popular preacher of the age, and his sermons are filled with lively anecdotes and quite common language.[20] In Latimer the priority of the oral sermon over written homilies began to come to the fore. Perhaps his most famous sermon is "Of the Plough," by all accounts a brilliant application of the Parable of the Sower, with its theme of God's Word as the seed, the congregation the field, and the preacher the ploughman: "[God] hath first a busy work to bring his parishoners to a right faith . . . now weeding them by telling them their faults and making them forsake sin; now clotting them by breaking their stony hearts and by making them supple-hearted, and making them to have hearts of flesh . . . soft hearts and apt for doctrine to enter in."[21] The issue of salvation for the hearer was at the center for the early Anglicans, and Latimer perhaps says it best: "This office of preaching is the only ordinary way that God hath appointed to save us all thereby."[22]

This emphasis on preaching, initially a defining characteristic among the magisterial reformers Luther and Calvin, took deep root in the emerging Anglican tradition. Edmund Grindal, Parker's successor as Elizabeth's Archbishop of Canterbury, was deeply convinced of the *necessity* of exegetical preaching. He even faced the wrath of Queen Elizabeth and subsequent sequestration rather than obey her command to prohibit "prophesyings," meetings at which pastors could improve the exposition and application of Scripture by conference. In his refusal rebuttal to the Queen, he informed her that published homilies were not an adequate substitute for oral preaching. There is no substitute for effective oral preaching: "The godly preacher is termed in the Gospel *fidelis servus et prudens* [a faithful and prudent servant] . . . who can apply his speech according to the diversity of the times, places and hearers, and persuasions are uttered with more affection, to the moving of the hearers, in [oral] sermons than in homilies."[23]

So when John Jewel took up pen to distinguish Anglican from Roman Catholic identity, his emphasis on the fundamental authority of Scripture for doctrine and practice, explicated both in written homily and oral sermon, was reflective of a widespread theological conviction that characterized the majority of Anglican leadership. The issue that soon arose around the emphasis in Anglicanism on solid scriptural foundation was how to prevent or circumscribe "private interpretations" and the "misuse" of Scripture. The safeguard for this turns out to be tradition, but it is tradition with a distinctive nuance—it is the "primitive tradition" from the first five centuries of Christian history before the establishment of the Roman authority (after Gregory I).

This linking of Scripture and the primitive church was central to the establishment of Protestant religion in England, and the sounding of this note was as consistent in apologists like Jewel as it was in the official formulas and liturgies of the Anglican Church. It is echoed in Jewel's *Apology* early on, when he lays out his strategy: "Further, if we do show it plain that God's Holy Gospel, the ancient bishops, and the primitive church do make on our side, and that we have not without just cause left these [Roman Catholics], and rather have returned to the apostles and old catholic fathers."[24] As he draws his argumentation to a conclusion, Jewel makes an interesting play on words and concept—the Church of England is not an innovator but a renovator: "And we are come, as nearly as we possibly could, to the church of the apostles and of the old catholic bishops and fathers . . . a pure virgin, spotted as yet with no idolatry . . . and have directed according to their customs and ordinances not only our doctrine but also the sacraments and the form of common prayer."[25] Horton Davies sums up the issue nicely by pointing out, "Not only was there useful guidance to be obtained from the undivided church of the first five or six centuries . . . the study of the Fathers was a proof that her firm intention was *renovation*."[26]

From Cranmer to Jewel and later to Hooker, Andrewes, and Jeremy Taylor, there was an abiding commitment to the primitive church tradition, but it was not a blind or servile deference to the authority of the Early Church. Much less was it a subservience of Scripture to tradition. For example, Bishop Latimer, while respecting the opinions of the ancient teachers, refused to enslave himself to them: "These doctors, we have great cause to thank God for them, but I would not have them always be allowed. They have handled many points of our faith very gladly, and we have a great stay in them in many things . . . ; but yet I would not have men sworn to them, and so addict as to take hand over head whatsoever they say."[27]

Thomas Becon, Cranmer's chaplain, was of a similar mind. If the primitive leaders varied from the "doctrine of Christ," he did not care a whit how venerable, ancient, or saintly they might be: "When Christ saith in the gospel, 'I am the truth,' He said not, 'I am the custom.'"[28] In short, the Anglican theologians were true to the Fathers as long as the latter followed Scripture as their primary authority. To put it another way, what Rome regarded as Anglican heresies, the Anglicans believed to be primitive orthodoxies.

At this juncture it is useful to pose a question about the authority of Scripture and the Anglican conflict with the Puritans. Did both not accept the authority of Scripture? Yes, but if the Anglican conflict with Roman Catholicism was over the interplay between Scripture and tradition, the differences between Puritan and Anglican were between Scripture and scripture. Both would have capitalized the word, but I use this device to point out that the Anglicans and Puritans were far apart on how to interpret the authority of Scripture.

The Puritans acknowledged that the Church of England had accepted the primacy of the Scriptures in its Articles of Faith, but they were also equally certain that the Anglicans had refused to follow the Bible either in form of worship or in church order. According to the "pure faith" the established Church had retained *too much* of the false traditions and accretions of Roman Catholicism. The difference is best described by way of contrast: whereas the Anglicans emphasized Scripture's normative authority for doctrinal belief and ethical behavior, the Puritans generally insisted that the Scriptures were an authority for more than doctrines and ethics—covering all aspects of ecclesial and personal life, and especially to direct life within the Church, both liturgically and administratively. The chief spokesman for the Puritans during the Elizabethan era, Thomas Cartwright, asserted that "the word of God contains the direction of all things pertaining to the church, yea, of whatsoever things can fall into any part of man's life."[29] In subsequent Puritan theology, this emphasis takes on a more propositional form. In a piece that proved to be of prolific influence through several editions, William Ames formalized the point: "All things necessary to salvation are contained in the Scriptures and also those things necessary for the instruction and edification of the church. . . . Therefore, Scripture is not a partial but a perfect rule of faith and morals. And no observance can be continually and everywhere necessary in the church of God, on the basis of any tradition or other authority, unless it is contained in the Scriptures."[30] In retrospect we can nuance these differences a bit more carefully by saying that the Anglicans utilized from tradition that which was not explicitly ruled out by Scripture, whereas the Puritans required a positive reference from Scripture. The historical point of fact is that the Anglican's felt need to respond to the sharply delineated Puritan perspective was carried out by Richard Hooker in his *Laws of Ecclesiastical Polity*. And Hooker's axis is a soteriological one, as he early points out: "In the number of these principles one is the sacred authority of Scripture . . . laying before us all the duties which God requireth at our hands as necessary unto salvation."[31]

The importance of this difference in perspective on the extent of application for the Scriptures, which all sides considered to be authoritative, can hardly be overestimated. It is a difference of perspective that carries profound practical implications, and Hooker was well aware of this. Was Scripture authoritative and normative for establishing doctrine and all things necessary to our salvation, or did Scripture carry a comprehensive absolute authority that carried beyond theological and ethical issues to judicial, political, military, economic, ecclesiastical, and organizational matters? Hooker addresses this axis issue in a straightforward manner: "Let them with whom we have hitherto disputed consider well, how it can stand with reason to make the bare mandate of sacred Scripture the only rule of all good and evil in the actions of mortal man. The testimonies of God are true, the testimonies of God are perfect, the testimonies of God are all sufficient *unto that end for which they were given* [emphasis added] . . . we do not think that in them God hath omitted anything needful unto his purpose, and left his intent to be accomplished by our devisings."[32] Through the Scriptures God has provided all that is needed for the salvation of believers. This is God's purpose, and God's purpose is the Bible's purpose.

To this point in our story about the emerging identity of Anglicanism's "middle way," there have been only two major components, Scripture and tradition—with an emerging sub-point being the emphasis on liturgy that can be experienced by a broad constituency. In developing his apologetic, Hooker adds another major point as well as a sub-point. His major point is the concept of reason, which remained implicit in the previous apologetic, and his minor point is the concept and use of "law" as a principle to help make his case.[33] It is very important to remember that Hooker understood himself not to be formulating a new theology, but rather to be dealing with the interpretation and application of the theology that had been given in Scripture, defined in the early centuries of the primitive church, and affirmed in the Anglican Articles. To say that Hooker was really dealing with *method* rather than the *content* of theology can lead to an emphasis that is methodical, even mechanistic, but we assume the risk of misapplication when we assert that Hooker's essential goal was to describe a viable theological frame of reference that would distinguish and define the "middle way." Hooker's apologetic is a culmination of the identity-defining process that began with Thomas Cranmer, and the result is a comprehensiveness of perspective that became an identifying trademark of Anglican identity.

As we noted above, the crux of the difference of opinion between Puritans and Anglicans lay in the definition of authority. Hooker attempts to avoid the horns of this dilemma by asking, "What is the source of authority?" His answer is "law," and in his thought law is an implanted directive. Law is reason—inherent, governing the universe—an inner principle that expresses itself by the fulfillment of proper ends.[34]

Although quite difficult to follow, there is a discernible logic and pattern to the approach that Hooker takes in developing his apologetic. It is not necessary for our purposes to describe the intricacies of his logic, for he sets out for us in his Preface to the *Laws* what he perceives to be the crux of the authority issue, and, in fact, uses Scripture to refute the Puritans' absolute authority position for Scripture by pointing out that their use of the Bible is not commanded in Scripture.[35] His point is that the very decision to interpret Scripture as absolutely authoritative in areas such as polity and liturgy is to beg the question. The Puritans chose the polity of Geneva, asserted with Calvin that this "platform of Geneva" best reflected the Bible, and so the Biblical authority validated their choice in ecclesial polity.[36]

It soon becomes apparent that the Puritans define law differently than did Hooker. Similar to their propositional use of Scripture, law means a prescriptive rule. This is not the case for Hooker. Law is not so much a series of promulgations as a pattern of characteristic behavior whereby all things are directed "in the means whereby they tend to their own perfection."[37] We might say this a bit differently but mean the same thing when we speak of a principle of coherence. For Hooker this set of principles is hierarchical and God is the first eternal principle or law informing the entirety of creation as "that which [God] hath set down as expedient to be kept by all his creatures, according to the several conditions wherewith he hath endued them."[38]

It is very important to notice in these quotations from Hooker the phrases about "their own perfection," "conditions," and "enduing," implying a dynamic interplay between creation and being. The result of the law is not a concrete set of facts that, having been set in stone, are amenable to being passed along unchanged. The result is rather a dynamic system that has pattern and meaning. The pattern and meaning may not be immediately self-evident, but will yield to the discernment of human reason. In this way the reason of the individual or groups of individuals may discern the comprehensive reason ordering the world.

This natural process is not separated from, but rather closely tied to the authority of Scripture. "It sufficeth therefore," he writes, "that nature and Scripture do serve in such full sort, that they both jointly and not severally either of them be so complete that unto everlasting felicity we need not the knowledge of anything more than these two may easily furnish our mind with on all sides."[39]

In this way the authority of Scripture is placed within the broader context of the created order. There is continuity between the authority of the Bible and creation, but the "laws of God" have logical and ontological priority to Scripture. This is the basis of Hooker's method, setting the question of ecclesiastical laws within the wider context, apart from which he believes that it can have no solution: "Lest therefore any man should marvel whereunto all these things tend, the drift and purpose of all this . . . [is] to teach a man a reason why just and reasonable laws are of so great force . . . and to inform their minds with some method of reducing the laws whereof there is present controversy unto their first original causes."[40] For Hooker this original cause is God and the primary laws are written in the fabric of the structure of creation. For Hooker and the subsequent architects of the "middle way," it is within this comprehensive frame of reference that all questions about authority must be asked and answered— whether the authority be papal, biblical, or otherwise.

Hooker's method may be crystallized, using his own words, in a few sentences:

> Be it in matter of one kind or the other, what Scripture doth plainly deliver, to that the first place both of credit and obedience is due; the next whereunto is whatsoever any man can necessarily conclude by face of reason; after these the voice of the Church suc-

ceedeth. That which the Church by her ecclesial authority shall probably think and define to be true and good, must in congruity of reason overrule all other inferior judgments whatsoever.[41]

As tempting as it would be to examine the relative strengths and weaknesses of Hooker's logic, and how this might or might not be instructive to a contemporary discussion, we must be content to point out what may be in principle Hooker's most abiding contribution, namely, that the issue of theological method is linked indissolubly with the "freedom of reason," and also inevitably with the visible Church. It is here that the work of Hooker, so influential in shaping the Anglicanism that Wesley knew, jumps across four centuries and addresses our contemporary setting.

"Freedom of Reason" and the Church Today

We have now for at least half a century had a tendency in too many places to separate the "freedom of reason" and the visible church. When place has been given to reasoning, a private use of it has taken us far afield, partly because the definition of reason that we have assumed is much more individualistic than that of Hooker and Wesley. Being aware of painting with broad strokes, but willing to run the risk, I offer the opinion that many have exercised the "freedom of reason" in theological discussion with little or no serious engagement with the visible church, except as the church may be said to be expressed in scholarly guilds. The situation is exacerbated by the fact that professional theological guilds have not only ignored but at times ridiculed the idea that the visible church should be a partner in theological conversation. But this sword cuts both ways. The space between lectern and sacramental table has only been increased by the lack of initiative on the part of the visible church practitioners to make the necessary effort to engage the scholarly guild in conversation—thus the false and fatal split between theory and practice.

These two were not separate in Hooker's days, although there were plenty who wanted to keep the "freedom of reason" out of the visible church. It is Hooker's genius that he wanted to keep all of this together. And in doing so, he set the compass in a virtually permanent setting to guide what came to be known as the *via media*. However, it is not a middle way really, if we mean by that a political compromise between opposed alternative views. It is, rather, a new

37

and different way. It is a way of theologizing in which the concern for connecting theological thinking with daily living required that the authoritative written sources of Christian theology be in a living relationship with the visible church (tradition and reason) producing an experience of divine reality that *graciously* gives rise to even the smallest beginnings of each.

In modern Methodism we have formalized this theological frame of reference and turned it into a formula. Perhaps we unintentionally capture and sterilize this dynamic when we "quadrilateralize" it into the formula Scripture, tradition, reason, and experience, especially if this "box" is perceived to be an equilateral. To avoid this dilemma of our own making, perhaps we should reconsider the contours of our parameters and return to a dynamic more appropriate to the Anglican framers and to the Anglican who gave rise to Methodism. We begin with the rule of Scripture, for it is primary. Tradition (the early centuries being privileged) instructs the church, especially regarding the doctrinal interpretation of the Bible. Reason, individually but especially collectively, elucidates God's way of being active in the created order. And experience, especially as religion *experienced* in celebration and worship, brings to life in the heart and mind of the believer the saving work of God in Christ. We of the Methodist persuasion are direct heirs through John Wesley to this way of theologizing, and so we look again in the chapters that follow at how Mr. Wesley theologized within the parameters of this dynamic. Mr. Wesley is not a final authority for constructing a viable theology for this or any future generation, but "the people called Methodists" would be well served to consider carefully "whence we came" theologically, in order that we might, with clarity and continuity, begin to define afresh where we are going.

Chapter Two

The Rule of Scripture

Scott J. Jones

A seminary student once told me why he joined The United Methodist Church: "I was in college and got acquainted with the campus minister at the Wesley Foundation. He said that Methodists were much better than my denomination, because you could believe anything you wanted to, and drink beer. It sounded great to me." It is important to note that this perspective on Methodist identity came from the campus "minister," and I am reminded that on several occasions when prospective members of my congregation have asked, "Do United Methodists believe in the Bible?" they had been advised by friends not to come to our church because we did not accept the authority of Scripture.

These friends had some reason for at least questioning Methodist commitment to the Bible, and we do not have to look too far to ascertain why. In many congregations our children graduate from years in United Methodist Youth Fellowship and Sunday school without being able to identify Abraham, Moses, Mary Magdalene, or Paul. When asked to find 1 Corinthians in a Bible, they start looking in the index. Many adults begin Disciple Bible Study without any comprehension of how the Old and New Testaments relate to each other. It is a common recognition in the seminary context that a majority of entering students lack even a minimal foundation of biblical knowledge, and this lack is not a new or recent problem.

In a *Life* magazine article written nearly fifty years ago, we read: "Methodism is long on organization and short on theology."[1] Have things improved over the last half century? Perhaps not. A 1996 editorial in the *United Methodist Reporter* describing how Methodists might work closer with a national men's movement reads, "The Wesleyan Quadrilateral of Scripture, tradition, experience and reason plays an important role in the development of ministry. . . . If [their] leaders become more open to tradition and reason and *rely less exclusively on Scripture* [emphasis added] . . . , they may expand their ministry to [include] mainline Protestants and Roman Catholics." And the editorial concludes that when all are included this influential movement will be able to demonstrate that its commitment "to demonstrate [that] the power of 'biblical unity' is worth struggling toward together."[2]

John Wesley would be appalled. To have a large body of "the people called Methodists" ignorant of Scripture and to have editors of official Methodist publications suggesting that Methodists can work with other Christians if they would use Scripture *less*, even if we said *less exclusively*, would have disturbed him profoundly, and would represent the realization of his greatest fear. In his "Thoughts Upon Methodism," written near the end of his life, he said,

> I am not afraid that the people called Methodists should ever cease to exist either in Europe or America. But I am afraid, lest they should only exist as a dead sect, having the form of religion without the power. And this undoubtedly will be the case, unless they hold fast both the doctrine, spirit, and discipline with which they first set out.[3]

When Wesley talked about the doctrine of the Methodist people, he understood that all of that doctrine was based on Scripture, and he had a particular understanding of what that is.

Official United Methodist doctrine still claims the authority of Scripture. United Methodists have neither formally repudiated nor modified the basic documents that outline our beliefs. The 1996 *Book of Discipline* makes clear that Wesley's *Sermons*, his *Explanatory Notes Upon the New Testament*, the General Rules, the Articles of Religion, and the Confession of Faith are still protected by the Restrictive Rules of our denomination's constitution.[4]

All of these documents taken together give strong testimony to the authority of Scripture in our official teaching. Thus, whatever United Methodists actually do (or fail to do!) with the Bible, our official doctrine says that it is important. But the current theological statement of the General Conference points to the complexity of the United Methodist understanding of Scripture. "Our Theological Task"[5] refers to Scripture, reason, tradition, and experience as the four sources and norms that guide United Methodist theology. Informally, these four have come to be known as the "Wesleyan Quadrilateral," despite recent academic debate about the propriety of the title.[6] More recently, scholars from within the United Methodist family have argued about the proper role Scripture should play.[7]

Scripture and the "Middle Way"

The Reformation slogan *sola scriptura* has power, clarity, and simplicity. Its power counters the authoritarian claims of church, later tradition, and all other competitors to the revealed Word of God. Its clarity shows others we are serious about basing all of our Christian faith and practice on this book of books. Its simplicity allows all Christians to understand the basis on which our claims to truth are made. We sing with understanding, "Jesus loves me, this I know, for the Bible tells me so."

John Wesley knew this and fully subscribed to the song's sentiment. When challenged on his most controversial doctrines, he appealed to the Bible as the primary justification for his teachings. In the famous passage from the Preface to his sermons, he calls himself *homo unius libri*—a man of one book.[8] Forty-one years later, he uses the phrase again to talk about the beginning of Methodism and its continuing commitment to Scripture:

> From the very beginning, from the time that four young men united together, each of them was *homo unius libri*—a man of one book. God taught them all to make his word a lantern unto their feet, and a light in all their paths. They had one, and only one rule of judgment, with regard to all their tempers, words and actions, namely, the oracles of God. They were one and all determined to be *Bible-Christians.* They were continually reproached for this very thing; some terming them in derision *Bible-bigots;* others, *Bible-moths*—feeding, they said, upon the Bible as moths do upon cloth. And indeed unto this day it is their constant endeavour to think and speak as the oracles of God.[9]

Any accurate understanding of Wesley's view of the Bible must first start here, with a strong statement that Scripture alone is the authority for Christian faith and practice. On this point Wesley is definite. It is the Bible that serves as the final court of appeal.

While Wesley is definite on this point, his position is not simple. The first clue to this comes with the phrase *homo unius libri*. Five paragraphs after calling himself a man of only one book, Wesley quotes Homer's *Iliad*—in the Greek, no less! Analyses of Wesley's writings show how much Wesley was informed by many different sources, not just the Bible. The Bicentennial Edition of *The Works of John Wesley* provides excellent pointers to the many non-biblical sources Wesley used. These include a wide variety of sources representing contemporary literature, classical Greek and Roman writings, and the Christian tradition. In one representative sample of Wesley's writings,[10] there are fifty quotations from secular sources, both contemporary and classical. Thirty of these are from seventeenth- and eighteenth-century English authors such as Milton and Alexander Pope, and twenty are from classical writers such as Virgil, Horace, and Plato.[11]

Furthermore, Wesley not only uses these sources to add to his biblical arguments, but he explicitly appeals to reason, experience, the Church of England, and the primitive church. Because of modern understandings about the importance and complexity of Christian tradition, The United Methodist Church usually speaks of tradition to include both of the last two. Hence, the Quadrilateral is used as a summary of how Methodists understand theological authority. To be faithful to John Wesley, however, this must always be understood as a single locus of authority with four unequal parts. Scripture is primary, and always interpreted in the light of the other three. For Wesley, all four terms are mutually interdependent. Reason correctly employed testifies to the authority of Scripture, and Scripture must always make sense. Not all Christian tradition is authoritative—only the parts where Christians were faithful to Scripture. Only those experiences where the goals of Scripture are actualized count in the theological arguments. Thus, it is thoroughly non-Wesleyan to play off any part of the Quadrilateral against the other parts, and particularly so if one part is used to nullify the authority of Scripture.

A few years ago a leader of The United Methodist Church was quoted in a newspaper article as saying, "I ran the issue of homosexuality through the quadrilateral, and Scripture lost, three to one." Such an abuse of Wesley's legacy makes two serious mistakes. First, it forgets the primacy of Scripture. Wesley could never imagine that any of the other authorities or even all three of them together could contradict the plain sense of the Bible. If each of the four could be weighted with "votes" on a particular question, Wesley would have been inclined to allocate enough votes to Scripture that its view would outweigh the combined votes of the other three. The second mistake of "voting" among the points of the Quadrilateral is that it undermines the very principle it seeks to display: the interdependence of all four authorities under the primacy of Scripture.

The Authority of "Scripture Alone"

When Wesley makes explicit appeal to religious authority, he most often mentions the Bible. A number of forms are used. In accordance with his rule of interpreting Scripture, Wesley occasionally refers to the Bible as "the law and the testimony," using the words of Isaiah 8:20. In his "Principles of a Methodist Farther Explained," he writes about those who have the right attitude toward God, saying,

> These need no outward miracle to show them his will: they have a plain rule, the written Word. . . . Through this they are enabled to bring all doctrines "to the law and to the testimony." And whatsoever is agreeable to this they receive without waiting to see it attested by miracles. As on the other hand, whatever is contrary to this they reject—nor can any miracles move them to receive it.[12]

This passage was written in the defense of Methodism against those who regarded Methodist practices as unreasonable and based on fanatical beliefs. Instead, Wesley argues that it is based on nothing more or less than the Bible. In the sermon "On Faith" he says this is true of all Protestants.[13]

In his writings, Wesley quotes Scripture far more times than anything else. In one representative sample of his writings, he quoted Scripture 2,181 times.[14] In the same writings, he referred to early church sources only fourteen times. His use of Scripture far outweighs both in content and in number his use of other sources.

It is fair to characterize Wesley's writings as embedded with Scriptural quotations and allusions. Sometimes he will string together many references, positioned in such a way as to impress the reader with the biblical basis of the message. Very few pages of Wesley's writings lack at least one Scriptural reference. Consider the closing section of "Christian Perfection":

> 'Having therefore these promises, dearly beloved,' both in the law and in the prophets, and having the prophetic word confirmed unto us in the gospel by our blessed Lord and his apostles, 'let us cleanse ourselves from all filthiness of flesh and spirit, perfecting holiness in the fear of God.' 'Let us fear lest' so many promises 'being made us of entering into his rest' (which he that hath entered

into 'is ceased from his own works') 'any of us should come short of it.' 'This one thing let us do: forgetting those things which are behind, and reaching forth unto those things which are before, let us press toward the mark for the prize of the high calling of God in Christ Jesus;' crying unto him day and night till we also are 'delivered from the bondage of corruption into the glorious liberty of the sons of God.'[15]

Here Wesley uses 2 Corinthians 7:1, Hebrews 4:1, 10, Philippians 3:13-14, and Romans 8:21. Out of 149 words in this paragraph, 104 are in Scriptural phrases. In §63 of *An Earnest Appeal,* a similar concatenation uses ten references in one paragraph.[16]

His uses of Scripture can be grouped into five categories: textual, explanatory, definitional, narrative, and semantic. The textual use of Scripture is familiar to anyone who has ever preached, read, or heard a biblically based sermon. Many of Wesley's 151 sermons are genuinely expositions of the text printed at the beginning. Each of the thirteen sermons dealing with the "Sermon on the Mount" is clearly based on the text. However, other sermons use the text simply as a beginning place, as does "The Means of Grace." Its text is Malachi 3:7, "Ye are gone away from mine ordinances, and have not kept them." The sermon uses the word "ordinances," beginning with the question, "But are there any 'ordinances' now, since life and immortality were brought to light by the gospel?" That is the only connection with the text. From there the sermon discusses other biblical passages to present the channels God has set up to convey his grace to us. While this is a biblically based sermon, it is not based on the text with which it is associated.

Second, Scripture sometimes functions as a way of explaining something else. If Wesley is arguing for a certain viewpoint, he might bring in a biblical text or story to prove his point. For example, when he is trying to explain his doctrine of perfection, he cites a passage of Scripture. In a letter to Bishop Lavington, Wesley is responding to the Bishop's suggestion that Wesley defines conversion in such a manner as to "start up perfect men at once." Wesley counters,

A man is usually converted long before he is a perfect man. 'Tis probable most of those Ephesians to whom St. Paul directed his epistle were converted. Yet they were not 'come (few, if any) to a perfect man; to the measure of the stature of the fullness of Christ.'[17]

Here Ephesians 4:13 bolsters Wesley's position that conversion and perfection are different stages in the Christian life. The quoted text functions as a warrant for the conclusion he wants to draw.

Third, Scripture functions as a sort of authoritative dictionary. Important terms in theological discussion are defined by reference to the way in which Scripture uses the term. Sometimes Scripture's use of the term is sufficient to settle the issue of definition. One of the most crucial definitions that Wesley draws from Scripture is his definition of faith. He quotes Hebrews 11:1 for this purpose at least twelve times.[18] Typical is this passage from "The Scripture Way of Salvation":

> Faith in general is defined by the Apostle, ἔλεγχος πραγμάτων οὐ βλεπομένων—'an evidence,' a divine 'evidence and conviction' (the word means both), 'of things not seen'—not visible, not perceivable either by sight or by any other of the external senses.[19]

Here, as elsewhere, Wesley turns to Scripture to define his terms. Once a clear Scriptural definition can be found, that often settles how the concept should be understood. Wesley was not simplistic on this score, for he could use several Scriptural texts to define the same term. For example, he could expand on the definition from Hebrews to include other concepts of faith as well:

> Faith, in general, is a divine, supernatural ἔλεγχος of things not seen, not discoverable by our bodily senses, as being either past, future or spiritual. Justifying faith implies, not only a divine ἔλεγχος that 'God was in Christ, reconciling the world unto himself,' but a sure trust and confidence that Christ died for *my* sins, that he 'loved *me* and gave himself for *me*.'[20]

The conviction of the unseen world includes the trust and confidence that Scripture elsewhere describes as faith.

Fourth, Scripture serves as a narrative storehouse, from which stories, characters, and events can be used as illustrations or allusions in his work. In *An Earnest Appeal* he writes,

> And not being suffered to preach it in the usual places, we declare it wherever a door is opened, either on a mountain or plain or by a river side (for all which we conceive we have sufficient precedent), or in a prison, or as it were in the house of Justus or the school of one Tyrannus.[21]

Here Wesley mentions the stories of Paul being opposed by the Jews and thus going to preach to the Gentiles in the house of Justus in

Corinth, or the school of Tyrannus in Ephesus. The stories are not recounted, but merely alluded to as providing precedent for his own activity of field preaching. It should be noted that these stories were presumed to be familiar to Wesley's learned audience, and that the allusion would suffice to press his point.

Fifth, Scripture can provide the words and phrases to make a point that could easily have been made in other words without a change in meaning. I have called this a semantic use of Scripture, because it is a substitution of words to take advantage of the authority associated with their source. The practice, of course, assumes that Scripture is understood to be authoritative. What happens in this case is that the use of Scriptural words gives an added dimension that is often unstated. This is by far the most common of the functions Scripture plays in Wesley's preaching and writing. In one sample of Wesley's writings, there were a total of 2,181 Scriptural references. Of these, 1,664 (76 percent) were of this "semantic" type. Consider Wesley's discussion of sanctification in "The Scripture Way of Salvation":

> From the time of our being 'born again'[22] the gradual work of sanctification takes place. We are enabled 'by the Spirit' to 'mortify the deeds of the body,'[23] of our evil nature. And as we are more and more dead to sin, we are more and more alive to God. We go on from grace to grace, while we are careful to 'abstain from all appearance of evil,'[24] and are 'zealous of good works,'[25] 'as we have opportunity doing good to all men;'[26] while we walk in all his ordinances blameless,[27] therein worshipping him in spirit and in truth;[28] while we take up our cross and deny ourselves[29] every pleasure that does not lead us to God.[30]

In this example, Wesley has made a semantic use of eight different passages of Scripture. Five of these are set off by quotation marks, but three are not. None of them is introduced by a phrase that identifies the passage as Scripture. Rather, it is assumed that these are known to be such. In semantic use, Wesley employs Scriptural words and phrases to make his point. The same content could be delivered in other words, but the unspoken message of Scriptural authority would be missing. It is important to note that Wesley's sense of the "wholeness" of Scripture and the comprehensive manner in which this informs his analogy of faith safeguards against this practice simply degenerating into exercises in prooftexting.

These five uses of Scripture are, to a large extent, reflective of the ways in which Wesley appealed to the authority of Scripture. Each use calls on Scripture to authorize Wesley's points in different ways. The textual use is a corollary to his decision to write theological treatises in sermonic form. Scripture forms Wesley's literary starting point in each case. At times it also forms his starting point in content, as many of his sermons seek to take a particular text with utter seriousness and understand how that can be true. The explanatory use of Scripture calls on the Bible's authority to explain other Scriptures or justify conclusions. In the definitional use of Scripture Wesley appeals to Scripture as the source for correct definitions that are crucial to the issue under consideration. Wesley's narrative use of Scripture reflects his appropriation of Scriptural and early church precedents to provide a rationale for his actions. The semantic use of Scripture is Wesley's way of giving his position or perspective comprehensive authority, for the words of Scripture are more weighty than non-scriptural words.

It is important to notice that Scripture functions authoritatively in at least two ways, as source and as norm. Scripture as source means the place from which the basic teachings of Christian doctrine are obtained. Scripture as norm means it serves as the court of appeal in disputes about what teaching or behavior is specifically Christian or not. For Wesley, Scripture serves in both capacities. As the source, it is the Bible from which we learn what God's message really is. As he put it in a letter to Henry Venn:

> I believe all the Bible as far as I understand it, and am ready to be convinced. If I am an heretic, I became such by reading the Bible. All my notions I drew from thence; and with little help from men, unless in the single point of Justification by Faith.[31]

Wesley's point is that the Bible is the fount from which our Christian doctrines flow.

But the function of Scripture as the source of our teaching goes farther. Wesley says that the Bible carries a message that the Christian is obligated to consider in its entirety. If the Scripture teaches something clearly, that should be sufficient to place it on our list of beliefs, whether or not the message is "comfortable." The Bible as a source of doctrine is not simply a market from which one can select whatever one wishes. Rather, he frequently talks about the minister as a messenger who is obligated to preach the message given him by the Bible. In his sermon on "Christian Perfection," Wesley asks,

> But are they [expressions that teach perfection] not found in the oracles of God? If so, by what authority can any messenger of God lay them aside, even though all men should be offended? We have not so learned Christ; neither may we thus give place to the devil. Whatsoever God hath spoken, that will we speak, whether men will hear, or whether they will forbear: knowing that then alone can any minister of Christ be 'pure from the blood of all men,' when he hath 'not shunned to declare unto them all the counsel of God.'[32]

Wesley is saying that the Bible is not only a useful source for finding religious truth, it is a mandatory source that requires the Christian to teach its message.

Scripture also serves as the norm for Christian thinking. When there is a difficult problem of Christian faith or practice, Wesley turns to the Bible as the authority that settles the question. It is not experience or miracles that prove what Christians believe, but the Scripture. In one letter he wrote,

> I conceive therefore this whole demand, common as it is, of proving our doctrine by miracles, proceeds from a double mistake: (1) a supposition that what we preach is not provable from Scripture (for if it be, what need we further witnesses? To the law and the testimony!); (2) an imagination that a doctrine not provable by Scripture might nevertheless be proved by miracles. I believe not. I receive the written Word as the whole and sole rule of my faith.[33]

When it comes to authority for Christians, Wesley frequently claims that the Bible alone has that authority. Other sources of authority for the Christian community must be seen as essentially related to the one, central authority which is Scripture. It is Scripture alone that is the rule of our faith.

It is instructive for us to survey the Wesley corpus and notice the way in which he frequently appealed to the Bible as justification for his positions. Two of his most controversial doctrines, assurance and perfection, are based primarily on his interpretation of Scripture. Consider his sermonic essay, "The Witness of the Spirit, II."[34] The text for the sermon is Romans 8:16, "The Spirit itself beareth witness with our spirit, that we are the children of God" (AV). Wesley's argument is an exposition of why that text must be understood in the way that Methodists have been preaching and teaching for the previous twenty-nine years. He begins by defining the term μαρτυρία as "witness," "testimony" or "record." He notes that there is no dispute concerning whether there is a witness of the Spirit or not; all are agreed there is. The issue is whether there is a direct witness or merely an indirect one. The most fundamental argument he makes for his position is that a direct witness "is the plain, natural meaning of the text."[35] He then considers the context of the verse, a parallel passage, and the logical considerations about how the various points of Scripture must fit together. Wesley has argued for his doctrine using a number of warrants, but it is the teaching of Scripture that is foundational.

The same is true for his teaching on Christian perfection. He claims that he cannot give up the word "perfect" because it is used in the Scripture.[36] But more than that, he reads the whole Bible as leading men and women toward the holiness that God requires of them. Many persons attacked Wesley's teaching on perfection as unrealistic. Wesley's response was to start with the Bible and show that the Bible demanded it. Of the nine verses Wesley quoted most frequently in his Sermons, seven relate to the doctrine of sanctification.[37] When the Bible teaches holiness, it is incumbent on all Christians to follow the teaching.

The Rationale for Scripture's Authority

The reason for Scripture's authority according to Wesley can best be summed up by a discussion of his closely interrelated views of revelation, inspiration, and the infallibility of Scripture. Wesley's clearest statements about revelation are found in his *Explanatory Notes Upon the New Testament*. In its Preface he says,

> Concerning the Scriptures in general, it may be observed, the word of the living God, which directed the first Patriarchs also, was, in the time of Moses, committed to writing. To this were added, in several succeeding generations, the inspired writings of the other Prophets. Afterwards, what the Son of God preached, and the Holy Ghost spake by the Apostles, the Apostles and Evangelists wrote.[38]

Three interesting points arise out of this paragraph. First, all of these words were taken verbatim from Johann Albrecht Bengel's *Gnomon of the New Testament*. Wesley acknowledges that material in the *Notes* is borrowed, but he still took responsibility for them by making the *Notes* a standard of Methodist preaching. We are not surprised to learn that Wesley's view of the process of revelation is not uniquely his. In fact, it is a view that was widely held in the seventeenth and eighteenth centuries, and indeed, most of Christian tradition before that time.

Second, the view emphasizes the divine origin of the words themselves. The content of the Bible is what God said to Moses, what Jesus said on earth, and what the Holy Spirit said to the apostles. This was then put into writing. The Bible is a trustworthy transmission of what God intended to say, because, ultimately, God is the author of Scripture.

Wesley's emphasis on divine origin is tempered by the third point of his position, that God used human agents in this process. There have been a variety of ways in which this process has been understood throughout Christian history, and Wesley never gives a complete statement of how he believes revelation works in Scripture. What is clear is that Wesley does not hold a strict "dictation theory" of revelation. He believed that God used human beings in the revelatory process in a manner appropriate to human dignity. This means that their personalities, their concerns, and their perspectives were brought to bear on how the message is communicated. In the combination of divine and human factors that produced the Bible, emphasis is clearly placed on God's assuring the truthfulness of the final product.

The logical corollary to his doctrine of revelation is that the Bible is inspired. The prophets, apostles, and evangelists were inspired individuals, and the words they wrote down are also inspired. In the Preface to the New Testament *Notes* he writes,

> In the language of the sacred writings, we may observe the utmost depth, together with the utmost ease. All the elegancies of human composures sink into nothing before it: God speaks not as man, but as God. His thoughts are very deep; and thence his words are of inexhaustible virtue. And the language of his messengers, also, is exact in the highest degree; for the words which were given them, accurately answered for the impression made upon their minds: And hence Luther says, "Divinity is nothing but a grammar of the language of the Holy Ghost."[39]

On Wesley's understanding, the words of the Bible are God's words. While he understands that human beings shaped the text and occasionally their ignorance led to problems with the text,[40] the Bible as a whole is inspired. God is the author of Scripture. This argument is made with logical precision in his "Clear and Concise Demonstration of the Divine Inspiration of the Holy Scriptures." In this brief argument Wesley suggests that the Bible must be "the invention either of good men or angels, bad men or devils, or of God."[41] His premises then rule out the possibility that good men would lie about what God had told them. The conclusion becomes inescapable: "The Bible must be given by divine inspiration."

This text illumines Wesley's strongly held view of inspiration. It is clear that Wesley regards the inspiration of Scripture as something so basic and so obvious, that it can be handled in a short three-point argument. In our modern-day language, he might say something like this: "Look, either the Bible is telling the truth or it isn't. If it is lying, then throw the whole book away as worthless. If it is telling the truth, then take it for what it professes to be: the written Word of God." Compared with more modern options, Wesley's view is a narrowly defined understanding of revelation. It presumes that a revelation from God is such a distinct form of communication that no one could be mistaken about its source. The premises of the argument say that a person knows when a message comes from God. If one passes on the message by saying "Thus says the Lord," either the person is telling the truth or is lying about the source. There is no possibility in this argument for persons who believe they are telling the truth but are mistaken.

Wesley's third, related characteristic of Scripture is its infallibility. Given the process of revelation where it is God speaking through the text, and the inspired character of the words themselves, it is inevitable that the words of Scripture are infallible. Wesley says,

> Nay, if there be any mistakes in the Bible, there may as well be a thousand. If there be one falsehood in that book, it did not come from the God of truth.[42]

When one is assured that Scripture is infallible, then what it says must be taken seriously. In his sermon "On Riches," he argues that the rich typically neglect Jesus' command in Luke 9:23 that all of his disciples deny themselves and take up their crosses. He writes,

> O how hard a saying is this to those that are at ease 'in the midst of their possessions'! Yet the Scripture cannot be broken.[43]

When Scripture is understood to be infallible, the difficult passages must be accepted and followed on divine authority. Infallibility is thus linked to authority. A fallible Scripture could be set aside if the hearers did not like the message. An infallible Scripture gives strong weight to all aspects of its message.

God's authorship thus provides a negative guarantee that the Scripture is free from error. It also provides a positive guarantee that the Scripture is unquestionably true, perfect, and consistent. At the same time, it lays upon ministers of the gospel an obligation to be faithful to the Scripture because it is God's word to his people. This extends even to using the words God had chosen, such as "perfect."[44] Not only is a Christian minister obligated to preach the commandment of perfection, he or she ought to use the word itself. Wesley concludes, "We may not therefore lay these expressions aside, seeing they are the words of God, and not of man."[45]

Nowhere does Wesley explicitly say that the Bible has errors in it. On this point he is quite consistent. However, two qualifications to this conception of infallibility must be noted. First, it is possible that some parts of Scripture may imply absurdity or contradiction. In these situations, a special rule for interpreting these passages is employed. Generally, the literal sense of Scripture is to be used. But if the literal sense cannot be the correct one, then an allegorical or metaphorical sense is the one God intended.

Second, there is always the possibility that human beings will misinterpret the Scripture. While Scripture itself is error-free, one is not always certain that one's interpretation has the same accuracy. Hence, the possibility for mistake is high, and it is almost certain that any one interpreter will make mistakes somewhere.

Wesley acknowledges that there are parts of Scripture that cannot be understood easily. He believes that the Scripture is clear in its main points. With other Protestants, he believes that the magisterium of the Church is not necessary properly to interpret the Scripture. However, he knows that some parts of the Bible are more clear than others and that one should use the clearer parts to explain those that are more obscure.

The Wholeness of Scripture

John Wesley believed that the Bible was whole. To twentieth-century people with theological training, this simple statement flies in the face of what much recent scholarship has done. Yet Wesley saw that God was the author of the whole Bible, and that it was therefore a most solid and precious system of divine truth. Every part thereof is worthy of God; and all together are one entire body, wherein is no defect, no excess.[46]

In many places in his writings he makes reference to "the whole Scripture," or to "the general tenor of Scripture." In Wesley's understanding, the Bible is a unit that is internally coherent and consistent. It has a message that is consistently given throughout the text.

This wholeness could be construed in many different ways. One might, for example, talk about the wholeness of Scripture as a history of a people. Others might think of the wholeness of Scripture as a narrative that may or may not have historical accuracy—a story that means a lot to human beings. Others might think about Scripture's wholeness from a literary point of view, suggesting that it uses the same themes and images throughout.

For Wesley, the wholeness of Scripture is constituted by its doctrinal content, specifically soteriology. The Bible is a unit because it proclaims the same message throughout. This message he calls "the analogy of faith." He uses the term eleven times in his writings, and one of the clearest statements about it is in the New Testament *Notes* on Romans 12:6. He writes,

St. Peter expresses it, "as the oracles of God"; according to the general tenor of them; according to that grand scheme of doctrine which is delivered therein, touching original sin, justification by faith, and present, inward salvation. There is a wonderful analogy between all these; and a close and intimate connexion between the chief heads of that faith "which was once delivered to the saints." Every article therefore concerning which there is any question should be determined by this rule; every doubtful scripture interpreted according to the grand truths which run through the whole.[47]

A number of phrases in this passage point to Wesley's understanding of how Scripture is whole. First, "grand scheme of doctrine" indicates that it is the message of Scripture that is consistent throughout all of its different parts. Wesley does not believe that God's intentions are different in the Old Testament when compared to the New. Nor does he believe that any book of the New Testament gives a fundamentally different message about salvation than the rest of the Bible.

53

The content of this message is God's way of salvation for human beings. It has three main points: original sin, justification by faith, and sanctification. At various times, he gives the components slightly different wording. His sermon "Causes of the Inefficacy of Christianity" lists the natural corruption of man, justification by faith, the new birth, and inward and outward holiness.[48] In "The End of Christ's Coming" "real religion" is described more generally as the restoration of humanity "not only to the favour but likewise to the image of God; implying not barely deliverance from sin, but the being filled with the fulness of God."[49] All of these are equivalent formulations of the plan of salvation Wesley sees as being taught throughout the Bible.[50]

Wesley interprets the words of Romans 12:6 "whether prophecy, let us prophesy according to the analogy of faith"[51] to mean that each passage of Scripture is to be interpreted in the light of this general pattern of its meaning. Thus, if you run into a difficult passage, its interpretation cannot be done in isolation from the rest of the Bible. The whole Bible ought to shape our interpretation of each passage. In modern terminology, we call isolating a single passage "proof-texting." The antidote is interpretation according to the analogy of faith.

Wesley uses this method in dealing with the doctrine of predestination. His Oxford friend George Whitefield was a Methodist who held Calvinist views of predestination. Whitefield argued that the atonement was limited to the elect, and that certain persons had been predestined to salvation. The Wesley brothers, on the other hand, urged that Christ died for all and that all persons have the opportunity for salvation. The controversy heated up in 1739, and John Wesley published his sermon "Free Grace." In it, his fifth argument is that predestination "directly tends to overthrow the whole Christian revelation," partly by making the Bible contradict itself. The idea that God would save some and not others is contrary to "the whole scope and tenor of Scripture" as well as particular passages like "God is love."[52] Other specific passages are quoted, but the significant point is that the entirety of Scripture is used to rule out a specific interpretation of certain passages. He goes so far as to assert

> better it were to say it had no sense at all than to say it had such a sense as this. It cannot mean, whatever it mean besides, that the God of truth is a liar. . . . No Scripture can mean that God is not love, or that his mercy is not over all his works.[53]

The problems of biblical interpretation are especially clear when we try to understand passages like Malachi 1:2-3, "Yet I have loved Jacob, but I have hated Esau," and Romans 8:29-30, "For those whom he foreknew he also predestined to be conformed to the image of his Son, in order that he might be the firstborn within a large family. And those whom he predestined he also called; and those whom he called he also justified; and those whom he justified he also glorified." How can this be reconciled with John 3:16, which says that God loved the world, and with 1 John 4:16, "God is love"?

Wesley's answer is that difficulties like this should be resolved by looking at the different interpretive possibilities, and comparing them to the general tenor of the whole Bible. He claims that the whole Bible points to the redeeming love of God and the possibility of salvation by faith that God offers people. Thus, no interpretation can be allowed that would contradict this general theme. "Better it were to say it had no sense at all than to say it had such a sense as this."

Another use of the analogy of faith comes in making an extension of a passage's meaning. In the Parable of the Ten Bridesmaids in Matthew 25, the ones who are accepted into the wedding feast are those who are well prepared despite the bridegroom's delay. Wesley's interpretation in the *Notes* recognizes the main point of the parable—the individual's faithful perseverance until Christ's coming. But his commitment to the analogy of faith leads to further interpretation of the details of the parable in an interesting way. If faithful perseverance means having a lamp with sufficient oil, what do the lamp and oil represent? Wesley notes that the foolish bridesmaids' lack of oil means they had "no more than kept them burning just for the present; none to supply their future want, to recruit their lamp's decay." He goes on to identify the lamp as faith, and a lamp with oil in it as "faith working by love."[54] While the parable by itself clearly teaches readiness for the coming of the Lord, the parable seen within the analogy of faith describes the way in which the believer should be prepared.

From the foregoing we may conclude that Wesley stands firmly within the Protestant tradition of interpreting the Bible. The Reformers established the principle of Scripture being its own best interpreter, with no external authority dictating how the Bible should best be understood. Interpretation of Scripture according to the "analogy of faith" meant that the whole message of the Bible should be used in interpreting its various parts.[55] Wesley understands, with other

Protestants, that Scripture is the rule of faith, and that its main message is the authority both for Christian teaching in general and for its own self-interpretation.

Wesley's Rules for Interpreting Scripture

Although Wesley never wrote a book on how to interpret Scripture, he does appeal to different rules at various places in his writings. These may be grouped into seven different rules as a summary of Wesley's views.

(1) *Speak as the Oracles of God.* Wesley says that whenever possible, the interpreter should use Scriptural language to express Scriptural ideas. His tenacious use of "perfection" was based, he said, on its being a biblical word. His frequent use of Scripture in the semantic mode is also related to this rule. In fact, the rule itself is a quote from Scripture—1 Peter 4:11 (AV).

(2) *Use the literal sense unless it leads to a contradiction with another Scripture or implies an absurdity.* In ancient and medieval times, four senses of Scripture were distinguished, two of which were the literal and allegorical. Protestant interpreters believed it was the literal sense that carried the true meaning, and use of the other senses was discouraged. Wesley was in agreement and said that most apparent contradictions between parts of the Bible could be resolved by a deeper reading of the literal sense. However, if two passages conflict or if they imply an absurdity, then an allegorical meaning can be used. In his comment on Romans 8:28, Wesley is again dealing with predestination in one of the texts commonly used to support the Calvinist position. Here he finds an absurdity in the portrayal of God "decreeing" anything. He says,

> Whereas, to take this consulting and decreeing in a literal sense, would be the same absurdity as to ascribe a real human body and human passions to the ever-blessed God.
>
> This is only a popular representation of his infallible knowledge and unchangeable wisdom.[56]

For Wesley, such an absurdity leads to a different interpretation of this passage, that God has eternally predestined (albeit on the condition of faith as a free choice) all persons to eternal life.

(3) *Interpret the text with regard to its literary context.* Wesley knows that proper understanding of a passage of Scripture requires that one

56

pay attention to its literary context. This means one must not "proof-text" but consider the whole book out of which the verse is taken, and indeed the whole Bible.

(4) *Scripture interprets Scripture, according to the analogy of faith and by parallel passages.* No external authority stands outside Scripture as its judge. Rather, the Scripture interprets itself. Hence, every passage should be interpreted with reference to the whole Bible. In particular, parallel passages should be considered closely together. Thus, the conflict between Paul and James on the necessity of works for salvation cannot be left unresolved. The passages are parallel because they deal with the same subject. They are problematic because they appear to be contradictory. Ephesians 2:9-10 says, "For by grace are ye saved through faith; and that not of yourselves: it is the gift of God: Not of works, lest any man should boast" (AV). James 2:17, on the other hand says, "Even so faith, if it hath not works, is dead, being alone" (AV). Wesley takes some pains to explain the ways in which these two texts are actually making the same point. Given his understanding of the wholeness of Scripture and its self-interpreting quality, it is a necessity that the conflict be harmonized.

(5) *Commandments are covered promises.* Wesley's distinctive teaching about the law is that God's grace empowers us to keep the moral part of the law. Thus, any commandment which binds Christians is also a promise that God will enable the believer to do what God wants him or her to do. Thus, Wesley interprets Matthew 5:48 as both the imperative and future senses of the Greek verb. Believers must be perfect and, by God's grace, they will be perfect.

(6) *Interpret literary devices appropriately.* Wesley knows that the Scripture uses literary devices and where that happens, the literal sense requires that such devices be taken into account and read in the light of their original intent. He believes that in Romans 7:7-25, Paul is using another voice to talk about spiritual conflicts that do not apply to himself in reality.

(7) *Seek the most original text and the best translation.* Wesley is aware of both textual and translation problems with the Bible. Modern textual criticism was in its infancy, but Wesley had learned from Johann Bengel the state of the science at that time. In a deeper way, Wesley's knowledge of Greek led him to make several interpretive decisions based on the best translation of a particular word or phrase. His *Explanatory Notes Upon the New Testament* gives a new translation to several texts, usually resulting in an improvement of the Authorized Version.

Interpreting Scripture Today

The question of how Wesley would interpret Scripture today hinges on two prior questions. First, what elements are so basic to his understanding that we cannot imagine him doing anything different? Second, what would Wesley have thought of the vast increase in knowledge since 1791?

We can answer the first question with some confidence. For Wesley, the divine authority of Scripture is so basic that it is inconceivable that he would change his position. The Bible is what conveys the word of God to human beings, and he would continue to rely on it as his primary authority.

Yet, to say "his primary authority" is also to invoke a second principle, which is that all truth is one for Wesley. He is committed to a clear understanding of a reasonable religion. In a famous line from the hymn "Come Father, Son and Holy Ghost," Charles Wesley writes,

> Unite the pair so long disjoined,
> Knowledge and vital piety:
> Learning and holiness combined,
> And truth and love let all men see.[57]

While John did not quote these words specifically, the same thought is expressed many times throughout his work.[58] It is characteristic of Wesley's theological method to claim a unity between all parts of religious authority. For John Wesley the Quadrilateral would really be one locus of authority in four parts. Thus, Wesley chastised his preachers who relied only on the Bible. We can safely assume that he would oppose the biblicism of later Protestants who pitted the Bible against all secular knowledge.

Wesley is also committed to a particular reading of Scripture. It is a problem for later Wesleyans that he never gives an explanation for why his version of the analogy of faith is the correct understanding of the main theme of the Bible. But the whole of Wesley's public ministry and personal life reflects the conviction that the doctrinal scheme of sin, justification, and salvation lies at the heart of the Bible's message. It is hardly conceivable that Wesley would change this basic reading of the biblical message unless forced to do so by other biblical arguments. In my judgment, no such compelling arguments have been advanced in the last two hundred years.

The second question with regard to manifold multiplication of knowledge is more difficult. During the last two hundred years a particular version of the Christian world view has come under attack by a number of new discoveries and forms of knowledge. The voyages of discovery in the seventeenth and eighteenth centuries found viable cultures that had non-Christian religions. Darwin and others laid the foundation for the conclusion that the world is older than the Genesis chronology allows if one follows a traditional "literal" interpretation. Freud raised questions about the psychological motivations of all human beings. Biblical critics raised questions about how the Bible was composed and emphasized the human origin of its various components. More recently, feminist theologians have shown that partriarchal cultural assumptions are deeply embedded in the biblical text. These and other discoveries challenge the basic assumptions that underlie several parts of Wesley's theology.

As an example of one difficulty in Wesley's stated position, his views on inspiration and inerrancy are untenable today. His "Clear and Concise Demonstration of the Inspiration of Holy Scripture" is overly simplistic. While the syllogism is logically correct (if you accept his premises, the conclusion has to follow) there are problems with the original premise. Specifically, modern persons understand that many times sincere people have said "The Lord said to me. . . ." They genuinely believed that God had spoken to them with a certain message. The process of revelation is subtle, and human beings are liable to make honest mistakes. In the twentieth century we see a range of possible explanations for a proposed "revelation" that Wesley never considered. In addition, the concept of a dictation theory of biblical inerrancy is seen by most scholars today as a theory that is completely divorced from the actual text, claiming more for the theory than the Bible claims for itself.

What would Wesley have done with such changes? Would he have followed the path of modern scholarship and accepted the benefits and costs of modern biblical criticism? Or would he have clung to the old ways of understanding the Bible and dismissed the new historical critics in much the same way as he dismissed the Deists and philosophers?

Our review of Wesley's approach to Scripture indicates that the heart of what Wesley can teach us is not fundamentally altered by the events of the last two centuries. Four hallmarks must be considered seriously if a modern approach to Scripture is to be accouted as

Wesleyan. First, the authority of Scripture must be maintained at a high level. Twentieth- and twenty-first–century Wesleyans should also be people of "one book." The current United Methodist statement about "Our Theological Task" properly emphasizes the priority of Scripture over any other authorities. Our Articles of Religion and Confession of Faith clearly state that it is Scripture alone which is the judge of theological truth. Nevertheless, Scripture is never completely alone. Including experience, tradition, and reason as vital interpretive components does not negate, but rather enriches Scripture's foundational truths.

Second, the general message of the Bible must be construed as the way of salvation. Others may argue that the Bible's general theme is something else, and such arguments may be taken seriously. While those who discern other themes may in fact be Christians, it is difficult to imagine that it is Wesleyan to claim any other center for Scripture than a soteriological one. At the heart of the Wesleyan approach to Scripture is the question of salvation, not only for the individual, but "the nation" and the nations. Given the maturity of the Wesleyan tradition, there will be a variety of different perspectives about salvation. Some will arise out of new readings of Scripture and what it says about the human condition, justification, and sanctification. Wesley clearly appealed to the Bible as his primary authority, and new biblical understandings must be taken into account for a view to be Wesleyan. Other perspectives will arise out of different readings of Wesley's own positions on the various stages of the salvation process. The long-running debates on gradual versus instantaneous sanctification have their roots in the writings of Wesley himself. In addition, modern approaches to the whole question of individualism in general must temper our appropriation of Wesley in our time. If pressed on the question, Wesley would never acknowledge that the individual exists in isolation from the community. Indeed, he said in several different ways, "The gospel of Christ knows of no religion, but social; no holiness but social holiness."[59] With these caveats, however, the point still remains. Wesleyan Christianity must, at the end of all of the process, focus on the relationship of the creature before the Creator, emphasizing the saving work of God.

Third, Wesleyan Christianity also must discern the process of salvation to include the doctrines of sin, justification, and sanctification. Wesley sees these as central to the "general tenor of Scripture."

To be Wesleyan, one does not have to subscribe to the idea that all of the Bible is a seamless unit. David Kelsey in his *Uses of Scripture in Recent Theology* distinguishes between the wholeness of Scripture, which must be discerned by every theologian, and the unity of Scripture, which sees it as one connected argument.[60] The wholeness of Scripture is its main theme, the element that brings it all together so that it makes sense to speak of one book. Other Christians are free to discern other themes; Wesleyans see the theme of salvation as this process of growth.

Fourth, some of Wesley's rules of interpreting Scripture remain essential to a Wesleyan approach. The rule that commandments are covered promises speaks directly to our theological understanding of the grace of God sanctifying those who believe. Interpretation according to the analogy of faith would be a helpful corrective to one modern scholarly tendency toward analysis that never looks at the whole Bible. Yet it is the Bible as a whole that is interpreted from the pulpits of our congregations and in the lives of Christian persons. Wesley's concern for the best scholarly helps in textual and linguistic matters also remains of great importance.

It is not essential to the continuation of Christianity that its Wesleyan branch continue, nor is a Wesleyan interpretation of Scripture the only legitimate approach. Wesley himself acknowledged in his sermon "Catholic Spirit" that our brothers and sisters in Christ have much to teach us on the matters of opinion that make up much of Christian theology. Thus, Methodism has long known that it is not the only true Church, but part of the larger, universal Church. Recognizing this, we remain consonant with Wesley's intention to teach and preach "the old religion, the religion of the Bible, the religion of the primitive church, the religion of the Church of England."[61] Our faithfulness to Wesley must lead us to a greater faithfulness, to the word of God as contained in the Scriptures. We have much to offer the larger Church, but it is imperative that we retain the sense that Scripture is authoritative because something indispensable is happening there: God is speaking.

Chapter Three

The Interpretive Role of Tradition

Ted A. Campbell

We live in an age of rediscovered tradition.[1] From Scottish kilts and tartan ties in charming little shops to African kinte-cloth scarves in tony shopping malls, late modern or postmodern culture seems to thrive on the vision of rediscovered roots. Sobriety suggests that this is mostly fiction, that our newly discovered ancestral cultures are as invented as microprocessors. But perhaps these invented cultures are only outward signs of a longing for deeper roots, which appears to be a very real longing. If the longing is real, it is real because of the massive devaluing and destruction of tradition that began in the Protestant Reformation and continued in John Wesley's age, an inclination that is still with us in many quarters.

In Christian communities the longing for deeper cultural roots has been expressed in recent decades in a renewed interest in traditional identities as Methodists, Presbyterians, Anglicans, Lutherans, even as Baptists or Pentecostals. These moves towards rediscovered tradition-identity often stand in an odd juxtaposition with anti-denominational sentiment, that is, we stand for what Luther stood for, not what Lutheranism now stands for; we stand for what Calvin stood for, not what contemporary Presbyterianism stands for, and the like.[2] The obvious analog for Methodists would be to say that we stand for a renewal of Wesley's vision that sits in an uneasy tension with the existing structures and institutions of United Methodism. A wide range of contemporary literature on the Wesleyan movement, including the current work, may be interpreted as reflecting just such a late modern or postmodern re-valuing of the Wesleyan tradition.[3] In this chapter we examine Wesley's own valuing of Christian "tradition" and the model it offers for the judicious appropriation of the deeper Christian heritage in contemporary Christian culture, as an interpreter of the faith, subordinate to the primary revelation of God in Christ that is recorded in Scripture, and alongside the secondary authorities of reason and experience.

Tradition in Wesley's Era

John Wesley lived in an age when tradition was both despised and revered. It was despised, on the one hand, by the enlightened *philosophes* of the eighteenth century, who tended to see tradition—especially the inheritance of the Christian Middle Ages—as a hindrance to the development of human learning. On the other hand, at least ancient tradition was revered by many in the "Augustan" age, and the architecture of Georgian England stands as a monument to their reverence. In a sense, the *philosophes* themselves had only pitted tradition against tradition: they had pitted the "enlightened" traditions of ancient Greece and Rome against the "superstitious" traditions of ancient Egypt and Mesopotamia, and of medieval Europe.[4]

Christian tradition, more particularly, was viewed with a similar combination of contempt and veneration. Protestants in general despised what they understood to be the corrupt traditions of Roman Catholicism, and more radical Protestants rejected all post-apostolic traditions as corruptions. And yet many Christians of the late seventeenth and early eighteenth centuries reverenced "Christian antiquity" or "primitive Christianity" as representing the pure faith that stood in contrast to later corruptions.

John Wesley reflected a similar ambivalence toward Christian tradition. His "Roman Catechism, with a Reply Thereunto" (1756; shamelessly adapted from the work of Bishop John Williams of Chichester) reflected a typically Protestant view of the corruption of Catholic traditions.[5] On the other hand, part of John Wesley's work of "revival" was his attempt to revive the faith of the New Testament, which he believed had been expressed at specific moments in Christian history. He had, then, a notion of what we would call Christian "tradition" that was in some sense authoritative for his own faith and practice.

Wesley, however, did not utilize the term "tradition" in the particular sense in which Christians have understood it in recent decades (at least since the time of the nineteenth-century Tractarian movement). In the more contemporary and ecumenical sense of the term, "tradition" denotes a normative understanding of Christian history, positively understood in some sense as the locus of God's continuing work in the world.[6] That is to say, "tradition" in our sense is a term that implies a normative content, and must be distinguished from Christian history in general. The term has not always been used in this sense: the first Homily of the Church of England, for instance, urges hearers to rely on Scripture, and not "the stinking puddles of men's traditions."[7] In that Wesley himself did not use the term in this sense, the Quadrilateral is clearly not his own construction, and a case can be made that in place of the Quadrilateral we should understand Wesley as embracing a five-fold understanding of authority including Scripture, Christian antiquity, the early Church of England, reason, and experience.[8] As we shall see below, Christian antiquity and the Church of England will be the two most prominent aspects of the content of Christian tradition for Wesley. In examining John Wesley's understanding of tradition as religious authority, then, we will consider his appropriation of the history of the Christian community in which he recognized some form of unity with the apostolic faith.

This examination of Wesley's appropriation of Christian tradition will focus on two questions: the question of how Wesley explicitly *conceived* of the authority of Christian tradition, and the question of his actual *uses* of tradition. Another item one might consider in this regard, though too complex for the present chapter, would be the question of the *influence* of various Christian traditions on Wesley, that is, the multitudinous ways in which elements from the Christian past were passed along to Wesley and so, consciously or not, affected his thought or practice. The study of the influences on Wesley's theology has in fact become a complex enterprise, largely characterizing what the late Professor Albert C. Outler called "Phase II" Wesley studies.[9] Although this chapter will not consider "influences" in depth, it must begin by sketching a general background.

The chapter suggests that Wesley conceived of Christian tradition in such a way as to highlight the purity of the ancient Church and of the Church of England during the Elizabethan period. It shows, further, that although he sometimes appealed to tradition in defense of existing institutions (this would be a more conventional use of tradition), he called upon ancient and Anglican traditions in a more distinctive way to confront the contemporary Church. This latter "programmatic" use of tradition indicates that Wesley and other evangelical leaders did have a concern for continuity with Christian tradition, in a specific sense, but did not regard *unbroken* tradition as a positive criterion in the way that Caroline Anglicans and Catholics had done.

Wesley's appropriation of Christian tradition should be seen in the light of more than a century of debate over the value of early Christian tradition that had preceded him. To take an early example, Bishop John Jewel of Salisbury, who figured prominently in the Elizabethan Settlement, had argued that Augustine, Ambrose, Jerome, Cyprian, and other early Christian writers should be regarded as "interpreters of the word of God."[10] Jewel's pupil Richard Hooker laid out a classic Anglican view of religious authority focusing on the interrelated authorities of Scripture, early Christian tradition, reason, and the authority of the contemporary Church.[11] Bishop Lancelot Andrewes of Winchester, writing during the reign of James I, summarized the Anglican position on religious authority in his assertion that "one canon, two testaments, three creeds, four general councils, five centuries, and the series of Fathers in that period determine our faith."[12] Modern studies of Anglican thought in the late sixteenth and seventeenth centuries have focused on the prominent role that early tradition played in the theological controversies of the period.[13]

But in the period that saw the rise of the Puritan faction at first within the Church of England, then the English Revolution with its polarization of Anglicans and Puritans, and its aftermath in the Restoration and eventually the Glorious Revolution, the authority of early Christian tradition was much debated. Although conservative Anglicans (like those cited above) defended the use of early traditions as a plank in their attempt to build a *via media* between Calvinism and Catholicism, a number of theologians, beginning at least with Thomas Cartwright, denied that early Christian traditions could authorize any doctrine or practice not explicitly taught in Scripture.[14] Anglicans of the so-called "Tew Circle" in the early seventeenth century sponsored the translation and publication of the Huguenot divine Jean Daillé's treatise against the use of early Christian writers in contemporary theological disputes.[15]

The late seventeenth and early eighteenth centuries saw the rise of Anglicans who appealed to Christian antiquity not so much to defend the Church of England, but as patterns for its renewal. William Cave, for instance, wrote his text on *Primitive Christianity* as a way of showing the virtues of the ancient Christians in the hope that they might be revived in his time.[16] Similarly, William Beveridge and Nathaniel Marshall wrote elaborate treatises on the canons and penitential disciplines of the early church, in the hope that Anglicans might revive these ancient Christian institutions.[17]

By the beginning of the eighteenth century, then, there were at least three different manners in which early Christian traditions were appropriated by Anglicans. (1) Almost all, Anglicans and Dissenters alike, utilized occasional quotations from ancient Christian authorities to refute the teachings of their opponents. Thus, Jean Daillé and the Tew Circle Anglicans could cite the early Christian writers in their case against the use of early Christian writings in contemporary theological debate! This "polemical" use of ancient Christian tradition implied no necessarily positive authority granted to post-canonical traditions. (2) Conservative Anglicans, especially those traditionally designated as "Caroline" divines, called on ancient Christian authorities to defend their Church's teachings and practices. George Bull, for example, defended the Anglicans' insistence on the Nicene faith in his *Defensio Fidei Nicaenae,* and John Pearson defended the episcopacy by appeal to the corpus of Ignatian epistles.[18] These might be classified as "culturally conservative" uses of Christian antiquity, and their uses of tradition tended to stress an *unbroken* continuity with the Christian past. Finally, (3) some Anglicans appealed to ancient Christian precedents on behalf of various programs for Church renewal, such as the works of Cave, Beveridge, and Marshall cited above, or the Latitudinarians' attempts to define a broad Anglican establishment claiming ancient Christian precedents.[19] These uses can be referred to as "programmatic" uses of Christian antiquity, and the examination of John Wesley's uses of tradition that follows will utilize this scheme of "polemical," "culturally conservative," and "programmatic" uses of tradition.

The Content and Authority of Tradition for Wesley

Although John Wesley did not use the term "tradition" in the contemporary sense, he did recognize a continuity with the apostolic faith in some parts of post-apostolic church history. In his 1777 sermon "On Laying the Foundation of the New Chapel, near the City Road, London," Wesley unpretentiously identified Methodism with "the religion of the whole church in the purest ages," which he associated especially with the church of the first three or four centuries and with the English Reformation.[20] Although in the last decade of his life he expressed his view that the "mystery of iniquity" had worked in the church ever since the New Testament period, he consistently maintained that the church of antiquity was particularly pure.[21] In this respect, Wesley reflected a notion answering closely to the sense of "tradition" in contemporary ecumenical discussions.

Wesley could appeal to Christian traditions broadly in defense of his teachings and practices: to Martin Luther in defense of justification by faith alone,[22] or to the rule of the Dominican order in defending the institution of lay preaching.[23] Nevertheless, there were two particularly prominent areas in which he understood Christian history as having a particular continuity with the apostolic faith. The first is, of course, the ancient church, at least through the early fourth century. The second is the Church of England, and especially the documents that came from the Elizabethan Settlement. The 1777 sermon cited above lays out this understanding in a particularly clear manner: Methodism, Wesley claimed, was in continuity with "the religion of the Bible, the religion of the primitive Church, [and] the religion of the Church of England,"[24] and in three successive paragraphs he explained in more detail what he understood each of these to be.[25] Similarly, in his 1789 "Farther Thoughts on Separation from the Church," Wesley appealed to Scripture, antiquity, and the Church of England.[26] In describing Wesley's understanding of the content and authority of Christian tradition, then, one must examine with particular attention his understandings of the early church and of Elizabethan Anglicanism.

The Authority of "Christian Antiquity"

John Wesley's views of early Christianity and its authority derived from a variety of interests and influences. His father had urged him to study early Christian writers and conservative Anglican theologians who had appealed to them.[27] While at Oxford, he came under the influence of a peculiar group of Nonjurors who stressed the authority of the so-called *Apostolic Canons* and *Constitutions*, and pressed an unusual program of liturgical and disciplinary reform based on these. These Nonjurors, sometimes referred to as "Usagers" because of their commitment to specific "usages" of the 1549 Prayer Book, were led by a Manchester physician, Dr. Thomas Deacon, who had been irregularly consecrated bishop in 1733.[28] Wesley would later write that during this period he had erred in "making antiquity a co-ordinate rather than a subordinate rule with Scripture."[29] His interests in, and appeals to, the early Christian centuries continued, however, as evidenced in his editions of the Apostolic Fathers and the pseudo-Macarian homilies, his editions of works describing ancient Christianity by William Cave, Claude Fleury, and Jean Fronteau, and his condensation of Johann Lorenz von Mosheim's *Institutiones Historiae ecclesiasticae.*[30]

Wesley consistently represented the early church as being the purest when it was nearest its apostolic roots, and as degenerating from that time, with a particularly precipitous decline in morals coming in the age of Constantine, when corruptions "poured in upon the Church with a full tide."[31] The following sentence illustrates Wesley's stylized conception of the early Christian centuries. Wesley states that "the religion of the primitive Church" was expressed

> even in the small remains of Clemens Romanus, Ignatius, and Polycarp; it is seen more at large in the writing of Tertullian, Origen, Clemens Alexandrinus, and Cyprian; and, even in the fourth century, it was found in the works of Chrysostom, Basil, Ephrem Syrus, and Macarius.[32]

As the last portion of this sentence indicates, Wesley acknowledged that in some areas pure Christianity continued "even" after Constantine, and it is interesting to note that his four post-Constantinian examples of pure Christianity were Eastern ascetic writers (and Augustine is conspicuously absent).

Prior to 1737, John Wesley had regarded Christian antiquity as having authority so far as it represented the consensus of Christian teaching and practice, and thus so far as it exhibited continuity with the apostolic church. Wesley appealed frequently in this period to the *Commonitorium* of Vincent of Lérins, with its insistence on the *consensus veterum: quod ab omnibus, quod ubique, quod semper creditum.*[33] A manuscript fragment of Wesley's "Essay on the Stationary Fasts" argues that whatever practices were universally observed in the ancient church must have had an apostolic origin, and must therefore be binding on all Christian communities.[34] This view of the authority of ancient Christianity concurs well with the interests in ancient liturgical and disciplinary life that Wesley had developed while in contact with the Manchester Nonjurors.

Although he never formally disavowed the importance of the

ancient consensus (it is implicit in his 1777 reference to the "whole" church in antiquity), Wesley's concern shifted late in 1737 and early in 1738, as he became disillusioned by his reading in the *Apostolic Constitutions,* and especially when he recognized that they could not reflect the consensus of ancient teachings and practice.[35] From this time, Wesley's references to early Christianity as a religious authority seem to be grounded more in his sense of the spiritual and moral purity of the ancient Christians than in their representation of a consensus of doctrine and practice. "I exceedingly reverence" the writers of the ancient Church, Wesley wrote to Conyers Middleton in 1749, "because they were Christians . . . and I reverence their writings, because they describe true, genuine Christianity, and direct us to the strongest evidence of the Christian doctrine."[36] The unity of the church in antiquity became one of the many virtues described by Wesley, and his editions of Cave, Fleury, and Fronteau all dwell on the moral purity of the ancient Christians.[37] This sense of antiquity's authority as lying in the purity of the Church's life accords with Wesley's general concern in the revival period for illustrating the "way of salvation," and especially the life of holiness.

The Authority of the Early Church of England

The early, constitutional period of the Church of England is the second source of Christian tradition from which Wesley consistently drew, and it is significant to note that his views of the authority of the Church of England shifted in a manner parallel to his understanding of the authority of Christian antiquity. Prior to 1738, Wesley reflected a Caroline theology consistent with his upbringing, insisting, for instance, on the apostolic succession of Bishops to the exclusion of acknowledging the validity of the sacraments administered by continental Protestant clergy.[38] During the period in which he was influenced by the Manchester Nonjurors, Wesley seems to have held an affinity for the liturgy of the first Edwardian Prayer Book, with its particular "usages" on which the Manchester Nonjurors had insisted (the mixed chalice, an epiclesis, and a preliminary blessing of the eucharistic elements).[39] Wesley's ecclesiastical inclinations in this period have been the basis for many works that have identified him as a "High Churchman."[40]

Evidence for a shift in Wesley's views of the Church of England comes from November of 1738, when, having returned to Oxford after his summer in Germany, Wesley "began more narrowly to inquire what the doctrine of the Church of England is concerning the much controverted point of justification by faith."[41] Shortly after, he published "The Doctrine of Salvation, Faith, and Good Works, Extracted from the Homilies of the Church of England."[42] From this time, Wesley stressed his allegiance to the Church of England as expressed in the constitutional documents of the Elizabethan Reformation, namely, the Articles of Religion, the Homilies, and the Book of Common Prayer. His 1777 sermon at the foundation of City Road Chapel claims that Methodism is in continuity with "the religion of the Church of England . . . as appears from all her authentic records, from the uniform tenor of her Liturgy, and from numberless passages in her Homilies."[43] Similarly, his 1784 letter "To our Brethren in America" holds the Church of England to be "the best *constituted* national Church in the world" (emphasis added).[44]

To the extent, then, that Wesley explicitly acknowledged the authority of the Church of England, it is clear that (at least after 1738) the authority he acknowledged was that of the foundational documents of Anglicanism, not so much the living authority of the Church as it existed in his day. He acknowledged this authority, like the authority of the ancient Church, because he believed that the Anglican documents reflected the purity of the apostolic faith. They reflect, he claimed, the same "scriptural primitive religion of love, which is now reviving throughout the three kingdoms,"[45] and he maintained that the Church of England is "the most scriptural national church in the world."[46]

Wesley's Uses of Christian Tradition

Wesley's actual uses of ancient and Anglican traditions reflect the authority he acknowledged in them, and display characteristically Anglican uses of Christian tradition. Like others, Wesley could cite ancient Christian authorities as off-hand barbs against his polemical opponents. Against the Calvinists, for example, he frequently cited Augustine's dictum that "He who created us without ourselves will not save us without ourselves."[47] Similarly, Wesley cited Anglican writings against his opponents, as on the occasion when he cited the definition of faith given in the "Homily on Salvation" against Bishop Butler.[48]

Defense of the Cultural *Status Quo*

Beyond these negative and sporadic citations, however, John Wesley appealed to the authority of ancient and Anglican traditions in a positive and constructive manner. Often this was done in defense of the cultural *status quo*. In this respect, Wesley corresponded to a more conventional Caroline (and Catholic) understanding of tradition, according to which "tradition" designates a more or less unbroken continuity of the historic Church with presently existing institutions and teachings. For example, Wesley cited Athanasius and the Nicene-Constantinopolitan creed on behalf of the doctrine of Christ's equality with God the Father against the Neo-Arians of the early eighteenth century (such as William Whiston).[49] Wesley's generally positive appeal to the Anglican Prayer Book and Articles is evident in his *Sunday Service of the Methodists in North America* (1784).[50] These uses of ancient and Anglican traditions support the general consensus of conservative Anglican culture in Wesley's age, against those (such as the Neo-Arians or more radical North American Methodists) who had rejected elements of that culture.

Advocacy of Cultural Change

Perhaps Wesley's most distinctive appeals to ancient and Anglican traditions, however, came in his insistence that Methodism was a "revival" of the apostolic faith that he believed was expressed in the Bible, and continued in the ancient church and in the constitutional documents of the Church of England. In these cases, Wesley's appeals to tradition were *programmatic*, since he appealed to tradition as a model for contemporary cultural and ecclesiastical change.

Wesley appealed to Christian antiquity, for example, as a model for personal attitudes and corporate institutions in the Evangelical Revival. He believed that the Methodists' proclamation of the gospel in a neo-pagan culture answered to the earliest situation of the Christian community.[51] He claimed ancient Christian precedents for the societies (the ancient catechetical process), love feasts (the ancient *agape* meal), and watchnights (the ancient vigils).[52] He called upon ancient Christian teachings to support what he considered to be the Methodists' distinctive teachings about the nature of faith as spiritual experience, and the elements of the "way of salvation" that followed from this.[53] He pointed to the faith, virtues, and holiness of the ancient saints as models for contemporary Christians.[54] Ancient

Christianity as a whole was portrayed as a model of belief and behavior, set explicitly against the models for belief and behavior that eighteenth-century Christians had inherited (that is to say, their culture).

Wesley's utilization of the Anglican tradition can also be seen as programmatic in many respects. This is surprising, in a sense, since one might presume that an appeal to Anglican tradition from an eighteenth-century Anglican would be, in the very nature of the thing, a conservative appeal. But the fact is that Wesley frequently cited Anglican documents and liturgy *against the* Anglican culture of his day. This is seen especially clearly in Wesley's claim that the Methodists had recovered an earlier Anglican view of justification. Wesley was convinced that many Anglican leaders had lapsed into a kind of Pelagianism or moralism according to which a degree of sanctification was necessary prior to justification.[55] Against this, he consistently pointed to the Anglican Articles and Homilies as teaching a more radical doctrine of justification by faith alone. This may be seen not only in his treatise on "The Doctrine of Salvation, Faith, and Good Works, Extracted from the Homilies of the Church of England" (1739 or 1740), but also in the long sections of the *Farther Appeal to Men of Reason and Religion*, Part I (sections II through V) where Wesley cited the Articles and Homilies in detail against specific attacks on Methodist doctrine, and in other occasional references in which Wesley indicated his belief that the Methodists had revived the doctrine of justification as taught in the Articles and Homilies.[56]

In such cases, Wesley's actual uses of Anglican tradition are structurally similar to his uses of ancient Christian tradition. In each case, Wesley worked with a somewhat idealistic or exaggerated view of the Church in these ages, and appealed to its institutions and teachings in those ages as a precedent or example for the renewal of scriptural Christianity in his own generation. The illustration of such possibilities would have borne considerable weight in answering the objection (or even the unspoken suspicion) that the religion of the *scriptural* age could not be replicated or hoped for in later ages.

There is a certain congruence between John Wesley's conceptions of Christian tradition and his uses of Christian tradition as outlined in this chapter. Wesley's understandings of both ancient Christianity and the Church of England were distorted or skewed in a way that supported his programmatic uses of those traditions. His understanding of the ancient church stressed the immediate post-apostolic period, not the more institutional Church related to the Roman State reflected in Ambrose, Augustine, or the ancient Councils. His understanding of the tradition of the Church of England stressed the Articles, Homilies, and Prayer Book, and it was easier for him to construe these as depicting an ideal state than the polemical treatises or edificatory literature of Caroline Anglicanism, since the latter had become the staple defenses of the Anglican *status quo*.

In this sense, Wesley found tradition to be a resource for the renewal or revitalization of the church. Just as Philipp Jakob Spener in Prussia had pointed to ancient Christian writings and to Luther as offering hopeful prospects for better conditions in the Church, so Wesley called on the resources of ancient Christianity and of the early Anglican Church as offering an idealized vision for the renewal of the church in his particular social and cultural context. The eighteenth-century Methodist "Revival" was, in part, a revival based in this vision of the ancient church and of the Church of England.

Re-valuing Our Tradition

Christian tradition can also be a resource for the revitalization of the church in our time, but we have to be very cautious, for the sake of honesty, about the extent to which we can idealize the past and our relationship to it. We face the temptation of constructing fictive, idealized cultures to satisfy our longing for deeper roots. Methodist people can take Wesley as one bridge to the whole Christian past, but we cannot find in Wesley a hidden path that leads to a secret garden of, say, Eastern Orthodoxy or Catholicism or even Anglo-Catholicism, for that matter. This would require an extensive denial of the complexity of Wesley's own roots, and an equally extensive fantasy about the relevance of Wesley's roots to us two hundred years later.

Following Wesley's lead in appropriating the richness of Christian tradition today must surely not mean that we should envision the Christian past as Wesley did from his peculiar situation in the eighteenth century. Following Wesley's lead today would imply our own critical appropriation of the Christian story, even as it has evolved since Wesley's time. It should entail a judicious reception of our roots in nineteenth-century revivalism, and an equally judicious reception of our heritage in the broad outlook of Protestant Liberalism. It might entail a frank recognition of the many points at which African American Methodists or Holiness folk or others have preserved the Wesleyan inheritance where European-American "Mainstream" Methodists have found themselves separated from their own religious tradition. Following Wesley's lead today would surely entail our critical reception of the inheritance of the Ecumenical Movement, and our critical reception of the Christian story as it has evolved outside the contexts of Europe and North America.

Given this perspective we conclude that it is inadequate if not intellectually dishonest for Wesley's heirs to look askance at tradition, view it pejoratively, and reject its consideration out of hand. Our calling then, in recognizing the authority of tradition in a Wesleyan sense, is not to favor an antiquated vision of the past; it is, rather, the calling to value God's own work throughout the story of God's people, and to take courage and confidence in the faithfulness of God speaking to us in traditions beyond the witness of the biblical age.

Chapter Four

The Instrumental Role of Reason

Rebekah L. Miles

When I was in college, my favorite pastime was talking theology. I waylaid students and sidetracked professors. I was dogged in my pursuit of religious truth. One evening in the school cafeteria, a friend asked me which of the four authorities of the "Wesleyan Quadrilateral" was most important for my theology. Buoyed by a new confidence in human wisdom and by my own growing knowledge, I answered, "*Reason* is the main authority for my theology. It's the final judge in any argument and the ultimate source for our knowledge of God." My friend disagreed, contending that experience had the prior claim. Within seconds we were caught up in a theological dog fight, blissfully throwing arguments at each other, prodding for inconsistencies, and hurling counter arguments. For me reason could be defined simply as the sum of what I thought about a topic or issue at any given moment, since I was most certainly a rather reasonable sort of person.

Only later, when I read John Wesley, did I see how thoroughly un-Wesleyan my arguments were. Certainly, Wesley was a passionate and unrepentant defender of reason. But *my* early allegiance to reason diverged from *his* on several counts. As we have seen, Wesley never focused at any one time on four definite sources (much less used the word "quadrilateral"). And, to be sure, Wesley would never have elevated *any* authority above the primary authority of Scripture. But my argument went against Wesley in another, less obvious way. Ultimately, Wesley would not have used reason the way I did; for him, reason could not serve as an independent source of knowledge. For Wesley, reason was limited not only by sin, but also by its own nature and role. Reason does not generate knowledge on its own, but only processes data and knowledge that originate in experience. It is a tool, not a source.[1]

Reason as a "Tool"

Wesley's perspective on reason as a "tool" was a by-product of the intellectual climate of his day, for he was influenced by the British empiricists, who claimed that all human knowledge springs from the data of the senses. The name "empiricist" comes from a Greek word meaning "experience." For empiricists, the experiences of the senses are the source of all knowledge. Reason's job is limited. It is simply a tool necessary to process data from experience; it is never an independent source of data. So, from a Wesleyan point of view, when I sang reason's praise at supper in the college cafeteria, I fell short—not simply because reason is subordinate to Scripture as a source for knowledge of God, but because reason alone is not a source of knowledge at all.

While reason alone is useless without data from experience, data alone is useless without the tool of reason. Without reason we cannot understand the data revealed in creation or Scripture. But reason working with data from other sources yields an abundant harvest. Reason reflecting on creation gives us sufficient knowledge to live and to work. Reason reflecting on ordinary experience leads to the accumulated knowledge of the arts and sciences. Reason reflecting on Scripture can give us reliable saving knowledge of God, provide theological constructs about God, and help us develop guidelines for moral behaviors.

When we say that reason is a "tool," we are asserting that for Wesley reason is an authority in a very different way from Scripture, experience, or tradition. The other three authorities are all similar. Though they each carry different weight, all three are resources from which to draw data; reason *alone*, on the other hand, yields no data. It is only a tool that processes the data from other sources. It is a necessary tool (necessary to understand, think, or talk about *any* aspect of knowledge), but it is fundamentally a tool.

This means that for Wesley, reason is more like a highly sophisticated computer processing program than the data that is entered. Both are necessary to write on a computer; but the processor alone, no matter how sophisticated, is worthless without the data. More homely metaphors will suffice. Reason is a pick ax, not the coal mine itself. A pick ax, no matter how sharp and strong, will not produce coal on its own; you have to take it to the mine and dig. And, conversely, a coal mine itself, no matter how rich and potentially productive, will not release one lump of coal unless you have a tool to work with. A pick ax will get you no coal unless you have a mine; a mine will yield no coal unless you have a pick ax. Thus, for Wesley, reason is a necessary tool, but it is not to be regarded as an independent source of knowledge.

Though Wesley never praised reason as highly as I did over supper that evening, he insisted throughout his life that "religion and reason go hand in hand."[2] The immediate point of this chapter is to explore Wesley's understanding of reason, especially its role in faith and theology. The bigger point, lurking around the edges of this chapter but only directly addressed at its end, is about us. What does this discussion of reason have to do with us today? How should we, as theological heirs of Wesley, properly use reason, especially in matters of faith?

Four questions shape this exploration. First, how important was reason in John Wesley's life and faith? Second, how did he define the word "reason"? Third, what did he believe reason could and could not do in human life? In other words, what are its limits and extent? Fourth, what does any of this have to do with us today?

The Importance of Reason for Wesley

You cannot read far in Wesley without finding evidence of his high esteem for reason. In hundreds of letters and essays, he championed reason. Wesley insisted that there was no "inconsistency" between reason and faith: "I would as soon put out my eyes to secure my faith, as lay aside my reason."[3] He never claimed that reason got him faith, but that reason was compatible with faith. When pressed to choose between faith and reason, Wesley insisted, "I am for both." He saw no inconsistency between them.[4]

Not only is there no inconsistency, reason is essential to the Christian life. A true Christian is a reasonable Christian. Any "unreasonable" person who claims to be a Christian, Wesley charged, "is no more a Christian than he is an angel. So far as he departs from true genuine reason, so far he departs from Christianity."[5] Wesley did not pull any punches. Reason is essential for religion: "Passion and prejudice govern the world, only under the name of reason. It is our part, by religion and reason joined, to counteract them all we can."[6]

When writing about authorities for religion, Wesley mentioned reason more often than any other authority except Scripture.[7] He frequently linked reason and Scripture together as authorities for Christianity.[8] Even when provoked by others in theological debates, he recommended that Christians "use no other weapons than those of truth and love, of Scripture and reason."[9] According to Wesley, this reliance on reason and Scripture was no new practice. Jesus and his disciples, Wesley insisted, "never failed to prove every doctrine they taught by clear Scripture and cogent reason."[10] Wesley often described the true Christian as "scriptural" and "rational." In a letter to a Methodist preacher in Maryland, Wesley wrote, "I wish to be in every point, great and small, a scriptural, rational Christian."[11]

It is not surprising that Wesley would value reason so highly. He lived in "the age of reason." Many in Wesley's day were thinking under the influence of the Enlightenment, a movement of the seventeenth and eighteenth centuries that *discouraged* reliance on the authority of a tradition, person, or institution. Enlightenment thinkers appealed instead to reason and experience. Influenced by this movement, many people in England during Wesley's life were confident about reason.

So, considering the spirit of the times, it is no surprise, at least at first glance, to hear Wesley insisting that Christianity and Methodism are reasonable. But if it is no surprise, if reason's powers were taken for granted by many at the time, then why was Wesley so emphatic in his defense of reason? Why did he go out of his way to insist that Methodists were rational? A defense, whether in a conversation or a theological essay, usually follows a challenge. Who was challenging Wesley?

Prominent leaders accused Wesley and the Methodists of "enthusiasm."[12] One might ask, "What is so terrible about enthusiasm?" Enthusiasm meant something different in Wesley's day than ours. The label enthusiast was not applied to those who were simply the eager promoters of a cause; it was reserved for religious "fanatics." The word "enthusiasm" comes from Greek words meaning "inspired by God."[13] At one level that does not sound so bad. Isn't the heart of Wesley's theology to be inspired by God or to have God's spirit within us? But in Wesley's day, enthusiasm was associated with fanaticism and irrationality. Some enthusiasts claimed to have access to God's voice through direct personal revelation. Critics feared that enthusiasts would give too much credence to the individual's fallible interpretation of God's voice and, at the same time, devalue reason or other traditional authorities (especially Scripture).

Samuel Johnson, a friend of the Wesley family and the author of a standard dictionary for the eighteenth century, described an enthusiast as a person "who vainly imagines a private revelation; one who has a vain confidence of his intercourse with God."[14] Enthusiasts were charged with claiming too much for their own religious visions. Wesley went even further, calling enthusiasm "a religious madness"[15] and the enthusiast "a madman."[16] For Wesley and other critics, a chief symptom of this madness was irrationality. According to Wesley, enthusiasts "despise and vilify" reason.[17] They suffer from a "disorder of the mind" that "greatly hinders the exercise of reason" and "shuts the eyes of the understanding."[18] Enthusiasts were accused, then, of being fundamentally irrational. In the age of reason, "enthusiast" was a fighting word.

So, Wesley's praise of reason often came in response to charges of "enthusiasm." He went out of his way to defend reason because he was accused of having none. Even worse, he was charged with promoting enthusiastic irrationality among the Methodists. One of the best known examples came from Thomas Rutherford, a well-known professor of divinity at Cambridge. Rutherford charged, "It is a fundamental principle in the Methodist school that all who come into it must renounce their reason." Of course, Wesley could never let such an accusation go uncontested. He replied, "Sir, are you awake? Unless you are talking in your sleep, how can you utter so gross an untruth? It is a fundamental principle with us that to renounce reason is to renounce religion, that religion and reason go hand in hand, that all irrational religion is false religion."[19] These are strong words. In all of these quotations and throughout his work, Wesley championed reason and challenged those who disparaged it. Reason is not only crucial for life generally, it is also necessary to religion, even to Christian faith.

Wesley recognized that criticisms of reason were no new problem. Even in "earlier times . . . there were not wanting well-meaning men, who not having much reason themselves, imagined that reason was of no use in religion, yea, rather, that it was a hindrance to it."[20] Though the problem was ancient, Wesley felt compelled to respond because he believed that reason's critics were growing in number, particularly in Britain.[21]

Reason played a crucial role not only in Wesley's theology, but also in his style, his character, and his education. John Wesley not only lived in the age of reason and valued reason, he was himself a man of reason. His upbringing and formal education nourished and trained reason. If his piety is known for its insistence on love and the feelings of the heart, his theological style is known by its rationality and logic. According to a later observer, Wesley was "a man whose heart was strangely warmed but whose head by inference remained untouched."[22]

Wesley's parents reportedly noticed this trait early in their son's life. According to later biographers, Samuel once said to Susanna, "I think our Jack would not attend to the most pressing necessities of nature unless he could give a reason for it."[23] John Wesley reported that his father once admonished him, "Child, you think to carry everything by dint of argument; but you will find how little is ever done in the world by close reasoning."[24] In spite of his father's words of caution, we know that the Wesley family cherished reason, knowledge, and theological reflection. Their regard for wisdom and reason is evident in their letters to their children, in accounts of Susanna's household teaching, and in Samuel's scholarly writings. Samuel poured many years of his life and no small portion of his family's scant resources into his scholarly study of the Book of Job. Susanna's method of home teaching aimed to form the children's "understanding." She later wrote that by breaking the will of her children, she established "the only strong and rational foundation of a religious education." The children then learned to abide by the reason of their parents until their own reason or "understanding comes to maturity and the principles of religion have taken root in the mind."[25] To develop their "understanding," Susanna reserved a time every week to talk with each child about Scripture, faith, and theology. With the help of their parents, the children not only learned to read Scripture while still very young, some of them learned to read it in *Greek*. So, even in the Wesley household, hardly known for irrationality or fuzzy-mindedness, John stuck out as remarkably rational and logical.

Wesley came to value knowledge and close reasoning not only in his education at home but also at Oxford University. His program for intense study and the lists of books he read and recommended all testify to the importance of the life of the mind to Wesley as a student. As a fellow of Lincoln College at Oxford he taught logic, Greek, and rhetoric—all subjects that promote critical reasoning. He recommended to students and later to preachers, his abridged translation of a classic text on logic. Wesley's close training in logic is evident throughout his writings, some of which follow the formal rules of argument and read like examples in a logic textbook.[26]

While logic was not the *most* important subject for pastors, it came close. He advised pastors that the study of logic is "necessary next, and in order to, the knowledge of the Scripture itself."[27] Wesley hoped that studying logic would help pastors develop their rational powers of discernment and argument. These were not secondary characteristics for Wesley. He wrote, "Ought not a Minister to have, First, a good understanding, a clear apprehension, a sound judgment, and a capacity of reasoning with some closeness."[28] To encourage the development of these capacities, Wesley abridged, published, and recommended hundreds of essays and books in theology, philosophy, science, and other academic subjects. The subjects required at the Methodist school at Kingswood included languages, logic, rhetoric, grammar, philosophy, ethics, and theology—all designed to train people to reason well. Wesley insisted that his preachers be well-trained; he was convinced that clear reasoning and plentiful reading would make for better preaching.[29]

We see Wesley's commitment to reason, then, not only in his response to charges of enthusiasm, but also in his life and character. He wrote and lived by reason. If Wesley's words flowed from Holy Scripture, the structure of his arguments evolved from Aristotelian logic. If Scripture formed the heart and soul of his theology, logic provided its shape and method. His style and personality were driven by rationality. Wesley was logic on horseback, reason enfleshed.

Wesley's rational, logical structure fit right into the Enlightenment era. It is easy to see that accusations of enthusiasm and irrationality provoked his emphatic defense of the rationality of the Methodists. But there is another crucial piece to this puzzle. Wesley argued not only with "undervaluers" of reason, but also with its "overvaluers."[30] Though Wesley went part of the way with the Enlightenment's confidence in reason, he could never go all the way. Reason's extreme admirers carried their praise of reason further than Wesley could bear. He complained that they "extol" reason "to the skies"[31] and even reject supernatural revelation as irrational. Wesley tried to find a "happy medium" between those who discounted reason and those who valued it too highly. He asked, "Is there then no medium between these two extremes, undervaluing and overvaluing reason?"[32] In looking for this "medium," he cautioned the undervaluers to recognize that reason was a "precious gift of God" that "directs [Christians] in every point both of faith and practice." [33] On the other side, he warned reason's overvaluers, the extreme rationalists, to "acknowledge that it is utterly incapable of giving either faith, hope, or love."[34] In attempting to find the "happy medium" between the extreme detractors and admirers of reason, he set out to define reason and determine its use and limits in human life. What was Wesley's "happy medium?"

Wesley's Definitions of Reason

We have seen that Wesley valued reason and defended Methodism as reasonable, but beyond asserting that reason functions as a "tool," the examples above do not adequately define what reason is. They refer to Wesley's love of knowledge, logic, and the thinking capacity. But what did Wesley mean by the word "reason"? When Wesley set out to define the term (a common first step in his arguments), he began by exploring the ways it was commonly used.

How is the word "reason" used? Wesley first examined its most common, flat-footed use. In this first sense, reason means a motive or an argument.[35] By this definition, when you offer a reason for something (whether an action, an idea, or a decision), you are simply explaining your motives or justifying your course of action. When we ask "What is the reason?" we are looking for an explanation. When a teenage girl challenges her father, "Give me one good reason that I should have to wake up early and go to church tomorrow morning," she is a looking for an argument or a justification. (In the case of a teenager, she may be looking for an argument of a very *different* sort. But *that* is another story.) We frequently use the word "reason" this way in daily conversation. "What is your reason for believing in infant baptism?" "Officer, the reason I was speeding is that I'm late getting to work." This is the most common way we use the word in everyday speech.

Wesley used reason in this manner throughout his writings, in both trivial and important matters.[36] An amusing example is his account of "my mother's reasons for my cutting off my hair." Her reason was that shorter hair was healthier. On the other side, Wesley's reason for letting his hair grow was that the barber was expensive. When mother and son offered reasons, they were laying out their arguments or justifying their opinions on the length of John Wesley's hair.

Though this meaning—reason as an argument or justification for our choices or actions—is one of the most common in everyday settings, it is not Wesley's technical philosophical use. This meaning does, however, lead easily into a key issue of modern philosophy—namely what is the most reliable source for all human truth claims, including those offered as justification for our choices or actions? In Wesley's day this debate had divided into two main antithetical camps—those who claimed that some knowledge came from reason itself and those who claimed that all knowledge came from experience, leaving reason as a tool or processor. Wesley considered the definitions of reason offered by both camps—reason as a source of knowledge and reason as a tool for understanding.

The first philosophical definition, which Wesley largely rejected, was reason as an independent source of knowledge. Some philosophers and theologians of Wesley's time used the expression "eternal reason" to mean the capacity of human reason to know the eternal or transcendent realm.[37] In the tradition of the Greek philosopher Plato, these philosophers believed that reason can find within itself eternal Truths that transcend our ordinary experience in the world. Theologians within this tradition believed that God created reason in the human mind and gave it certain knowledge so that it could have access to the divine mind. Ideas of God and truth are implanted within the mind or written on the heart. These "innate" ideas are a *given*; they do not depend on any experience or special revelation. Reason can know these Truths about the essential nature of God independently, without additional input from the senses or from revelation. This argument found many admirers in Wesley's day.

Many scholars agree that Wesley rejected this Platonic definition of reason.[38] Wesley dismissed the tradition of eternal reason, writing that it was a "flat contradiction."[39] He objected to those who claimed that God "stamped . . . an idea of himself on every human soul." Wesley contended,

No man ever did, or does now find any such idea stamped upon his soul. The little which we do know of God (except what we receive by the inspiration of the Holy One) we do not gather from an inward impression, but gradually from without. 'The invisible things of God', if they are known at all, 'are known from the things

85

that are made;' not from what God hath written on our hearts, but from what he hath written in all his works.[40]

So, any universal human knowledge of God is derived not from innate ideas "written on our hearts," but from the data of creation "written in all his works." (For Wesley, the *primary* source for knowledge about God is, of course, Scripture.) Our knowledge depends not on reason alone but on reason interacting with external data from experience.

Having rejected the first philosophical definition of eternal reason or reason as a source of knowledge, Wesley championed the second—reason as a tool or capacity for understanding. In Wesley's British setting (especially at Oxford) this empirical definition of reason was the common alternative to reason as an independent source of knowledge. Here, experience, not reason, is the primary source of human knowledge. Reason is simply a tool or a "faculty of the soul" (the mind) for understanding and working with data.[41] This definition, seen throughout Wesley's work, was common among British empiricists who saw themselves in the tradition of the Greek philosopher Aristotle. For these empiricists, Wesley included, the mind has no innate ideas; human reason has no direct, unmediated access to the eternal realm but has a limited role as a processor or tool working with experience. Wesley wrote, "All the knowledge which we naturally have is originally derived from our senses." Even that knowledge which seems "so plain and obvious that we can very hardly avoid knowing them as soon as we come to the use of our understanding; yet the knowledge even of those is not innate, but derived from some of our senses."[42] For empiricists, reason has a much less grand role than for the Platonists; it simply processes information or data derived from other sources. The point to remember is that for Wesley and other empiricists, reason is a tool, not an independent source for knowledge. It is the pick, not the coal mine itself. This Aristotelian empiricist version of reason was diametrically opposed to the Platonist view. But as we will see below, Wesley developed an empiricist model with a Platonic twist.

How does reason function in Wesley's empirical model? For Wesley, reason was a capacity or "faculty of the soul" with three operations or ways of working. It "exerts itself in three ways: by simple apprehension, by judgment, and by discourse."[43] The first operation or task of the understanding, "simple apprehension," is the most basic. Reason at this stage simply notices or takes in the information or data presented. Wesley wrote that apprehension means "barely conceiving a thing in the mind, the first and most simple act of understanding."[44] For example, I see a car in the parking lot of the grocery store and simply register its presence in my mind before thinking much about it or noticing that it is similar to my sister's car. In the first operation of reason, I simply apprehend or take in the idea or the sense data.

In the second operation or task of human understanding, called "judgment," reason begins to think with the various impressions from the senses. It processes the new data in relation to the old data, comparing, contrasting, and judging. For Wesley, judgment is "determining that the things before conceived either agree with or differ from each other."[45] In this stage, reason sorts and categorizes the new data in relation to other data. I not only see the car but recognize that it is similar to my sister's car. I notice too that the paint is peeling off the hood of this car in a way that I never noticed on my sister's car. In the second operation, I begin to work with the various data through comparison and contrast with previous data.

And finally, in the operation or task that Wesley called "discourse," the mind begins to think actively with the data. Wesley defined the operation of discourse as the "motion of the progress of the mind from one judgment to another."[46] In this stage, reason not only sorts and categorizes the new data with old data, but thinks with the data. In conversation with others or in the discourse of our own minds, we carry the ideas farther. We not only compare two ideas, but also think of a third mediating idea. We not only see what exists in the world, but also imagine alternatives. We not only note the differences between two theories, but also recognize their internal weaknesses and develop strategies to avoid those problems.

Returning to our practical example, I not only notice the car in the parking lot and compare it with my sister's car, but I ask myself if the paint on my sister's car is also damaged or prone to peeling. I wonder what might have caused this problem and what my sister could do to protect the paint on *her* car. If I make cars for a living (or especially if I manufacture car paint), I might try to discover why the paint was damaged. I might think about how to develop better paints or more reliable systems of application. If, while I am looking at the car, the owner walks up, pushing a full grocery cart, he and I might talk together about the damaged paint as he empties the groceries into his vehicle. As I talk with myself and with him about the problem, I have moved into a much more complex level of thinking.

All of these operations or tasks (apprehension, judgment, and discourse) are a part of reason's work. The later tasks are built on the first task of simple apprehension. The most complex workings of reason depend on the simpler task of taking in data through the senses. Reason does not find ideas innate within itself but always works from the earlier data of the senses.

While most theological debates emerge at the more complex level of discourse, they depend on the simpler operation of basic understanding or apprehension. Before we ever reach the point of talking about the complexities of original sin, for example, we first see the evidence of sin in the world—in newspapers, at our work, on the playground, and in our own hearts. We think about what is wrong and right with human beings. We read or hear about different theories. We compare and contrast experiences and theories. In a meaningful discussion of original sin, we build on our own previous apprehension, judgment, and discourse. We also build on the prior apprehension, judgment, and discourse of others—of fifth century theologians, the writers of Scripture, Sunday school teachers, and our parents, for example. But ultimately, all knowledge begins not with innate ideas, but with sense experience, whether ours or someone else's.

Wesley repeatedly described reason as a faculty of the soul for understanding, as a processor with three operations.[47] Though Wesley believed that this definition best described the actual workings of the human mind, he did not stay up late at night inventing the definition himself or finding it innately written on his own heart. Wesley inherited this model of reason from the Aristotelian logical tradition that he learned at Oxford and, particularly, from his reading of the logician Henry Aldrich, whose work Wesley had translated and taught.[48]

In Wesley's day, the Cambridge Platonists and the Oxford Aristotelians (empiricists) offered two conflicting views of human reason. Though Wesley ultimately sided with the empiricists, he also incorporated some aspects of the Platonists. He worked out his own empiricist "happy medium" between the two options. Because this debate was so crucial to Wesley's arguments about reason, we need to look further at the tensions between Platonists and Aristotelians. As we saw above, the Platonists (including the Cambridge Platonists) thought that reason could discern ideas innate within the human mind and thereby know something of the transcendent realm. Some claimed that God had written these ideas on human hearts. The empirical Oxford Aristotelians, on the other hand, rejected innate ideas and insisted that all knowledge comes from sense experience.[49]

While these empiricist ideas may seem strange at first, they are easy to understand precisely because they ring true to our most ordinary interactions in the world. Before we gain formal knowledge about cottonwood trees or mulberries, for example, we experience them. We smell, touch, and climb the cottonwood. We see, pick, and taste the mulberry. We are not born with knowledge of cottonwood trees. And knowledge of mulberries will not automatically emerge from the processes of reason. A child, not having seen or heard of a mulberry, could sit and think all day and all night long, concentrating as hard as he could, but would never come up with one bit of knowledge about a mulberry. That knowledge comes only from an encounter with a mulberry. If the child does not see the mulberry for himself, he at least looks at a picture or hears his big sister's report of *her* encounter with a mulberry. This empiricist claim rings true to our ordinary experience.

Empiricists insist that *all* human knowledge, not just knowledge of mulberries and cottonwoods, begins with our experience. For Wesley, even our knowledge of God comes from experience. A scholar could sit in a study all day and all night long, concentrating as hard as she could, and still not come up with much knowledge about God. (Granted, she might come up with a *little* knowledge of God, because God is everywhere, even in the study and in her own experience. The *mulberry's* location, on the other hand, is more clearly circumscribed.) The point is that the mind or reason alone does not generate knowledge of God. We come to know about God through the evidence of God's creation, through our experience of Scripture, and through our own spiritual senses.[50] Reason's task is simply to reflect on and think with experience. It cannot produce any data on its own, discover truths from unquestionable first principles, or find ideas innate within the mind. Instead, reason always relies on outside data derived from the senses. Empiricists insist that reason's task is simply to understand, process, and think with data first received from everyday experience—from cottonwood trees, from mulberries, and from other avenues accessible to our senses.

Wesley often recalled a favorite empiricist quotation. He wrote,

Nihil est in intellectu quod non fuit prius in sensu. In plain English that means, "Nothing is in the understanding, which was not first perceived by the senses."[51] Or in plainer English still, "There are no mulberries in the understanding, that were not first perceived (seen, touched, tasted) by the senses." (Or, best of all, "There are no mulberries in the mind, that were not first in the mouth.")

In stark contrast, the Platonists believe, to continue with our concrete example, not only that the *idea* of the mulberry exists in the divine and human mind independently of the physical mulberry, but also that the idea of the mulberry is prior to the physical mulberry. The mulberry in the mind takes precedence over the mulberry in the mouth. Of course, the Platonists are not claiming that if we just think hard enough, we will discover the *idea* of the mulberry without ever having seen or heard of an actual mulberry. They are arguing, instead, that the *idea* of the mulberry, which exists in the divine mind independently of our experience, is more real than the physical mulberry. When we first taste of the physical mulberry, we are somehow participating in or discovering something that already existed. Speaking theologically, our reason has within it certain ideas about God, human nature, and morality. When we first "learn" or "experience" these things, we experience them as "discovery." These ideas are "discovered" because they are already within us innately or written on our hearts.

Of course, the real issue in Wesley's day was not about human experience of mulberries. One of the major objections in religious circles to empiricist approaches was that God cannot be "experienced" in the same way that we experience trees and mulberries. This led some thinkers (especially the Cambridge Platonists) to turn instead to the claim that knowledge of God was innate in reason (reason being our participation in God's own rationality!). Some scholars have sensed sympathy in Wesley's uses of "reason" for this rationalist camp.[52] But, as we saw above, Wesley sharply dismissed this tradition and worked more consistently from an empiricist model.

For the empiricists, no ideas about God (or anything else) are innately written on our hearts or implanted in our reason. Many empiricists were skeptical about the possibility of *any* human knowledge of God that went beyond the evidence from the ordinary, physical senses. But Wesley parted company with these skeptical empiricists. How does Wesley deal with knowledge of God in his empirical framework? Because Wesley believed in the spiritual senses, he was convinced that believers could have some limited access, through these senses, to a transcendent or spiritual realm. As we will see, Wesley's ideas of spiritual senses allowed him to stay within his empiricist model while appearing more Platonic.

Wesley believed that God had given the spiritual senses to all people through the additional gift of restored grace. But the "eyes" of the spiritual senses are opened in the believer only by the work of the Holy Spirit. Though all have the eyes of the spiritual senses, not all can see. Wesley explains the spiritual senses with an illustration from nature. Imagine a toad trapped inside the hollow space in a huge tree for over a century.[53] (Wesley, however reasonable, is stretching the limits of *our* reason here.) The toad has eyes, but cannot see. Trapped in total darkness, the toad's natural sense of vision is useless. And because its vision and other senses are blocked by its captivity in the tree, the toad is not only "destitute of sensation," but therefore "equally destitute of reflection."[54] Only when the ax of a logger splits open the tree, releasing light into the hollow space, does the toad see and hear. The toad's senses existed in the darkness, but could only work after the blows of the ax exposed its ears and eyes to the air and light.

Wesley compared those who "exist without God" to the toad that exists in darkness. "A thick veil is between [the atheist] and the invisible world." Though the unbelievers have all spiritual senses, they cannot use them. What will rend the veil that separates the unbeliever from the invisible world? Wesley insisted that the spiritual senses, present in all through prevenient grace, are made effective only through the work of the Holy Spirit in the believer.

> But the moment the Spirit of the Almighty strikes the heart of him that was till then without God in the world, it breaks the hardness of his heart, and creates all things new. . . . He sees, so far as his newly-opened eyes can bear the sight. . . . By the same gracious stroke, he that before had ears, but heard not, is now made capable of hearing. He hears . . . the voice of him that is the 'resurrection and the life.' At the same time, he receives other spiritual senses capable of discerning spiritual good and evil. He is enabled to taste, as well as to see, how gracious the Lord is.[55]

Through these newly opened senses, believers see, hear, and taste the spiritual realm. They know and feel the presence of God. As extraordinary as this new sight is, human vision will be made even sharper in eternity. In heaven, new senses will be opened. In Wesley's last written sermon, dated a month and a half before his death, he wondered what his senses would be like when he no longer had a body. "When my eyes no longer transmit the rays of light, how will the naked spirit *see*? When the organs of hearing are mouldered into dust, in what manner shall I *hear*?"[56] He suggests that humans will be given "senses of a different nature." "What astonishing scenes will then discover themselves to our newly opening sense!" Most important, with these new senses, we will "feel ourselves swallowed up of him who is in this and every place."[57] In eternity, we will see and feel the all-encompassing presence of God to the fullness of which we are now blind and numb. So, for Wesley, even in eternity, our knowledge and experience of God come from our senses. Even as he experiences the deterioration of his own physical senses, he looks toward the giving and opening of new senses. With the new senses given in eternity, reason will have an abundance of data and will come to greater knowledge. Thus, Wesley's empiricist view of the world endured even into eternity.

What is the significance of these spiritual senses for our discussion? These spiritual senses helped Wesley partially reconcile the disagreements between the Cambridge Platonists and the Oxford Aristotelian empiricists. Because Wesley believed in the *spiritual senses*, he could remain an empiricist, insisting on reason's dependence on experience, while still claiming that humans could have direct knowledge of the spiritual realm.[58] The spiritual senses allowed Wesley to unite his empiricist method with Platonic ends. He developed what we might call a "transcendental empiricism."[59]

The main point to remember is that Wesley rejected the Platonic idea of eternal reason. Reason has no direct, independent access to divine truth. Wesley sided, instead, with the Aristotelian empiricists. Reason processes data received from the senses. Ultimately, then, Wesley is still an empiricist. Reason only acts on information received from the senses. But Wesley's notion of the spiritual senses blurs the old lines between Platonists and Aristotelians. Because we have spiritual senses, we can perceive, through faith and the work of the Holy Spirit, the spiritual realm. By including spiritual senses in his empiricist framework, Wesley came to a similar end result as the Platonists, but by very different means. The believer comes to know the eternal not through reason and innate ideas, but through the senses, the spiritual senses. The resulting knowledge looks Platonic because we have real access to the transcendent realm. But Wesley came to that Platonic end by strictly empiricist means—by the immediate experience of the senses. Wesley's "happy medium" is still an empiricist way, but his Aristotelian empiricist way leads to a Platonic destination.

I have argued here that Wesley's empiricist model understood reason to have a limited role as a tool. However, there are occasions when Wesley seemed to make more grand claims for reason. Wesley sometimes used the word "reason" to mean "common sense" or the general, obvious conclusions of reasoning.[60] We might say, "Reason tells us that a dozen toddlers left unsupervised in the church sanctuary will likely get into trouble." If you push to discover the meaning behind the word "reason" here, it boils down to a pragmatic, common sense wisdom that many would accept. Wesley often appealed to reason in this broad sense to explain or justify a conclusion or a decision. At times he used the word "reason" to refer to conclusions that *any* reasonable person would accept.[61] Someone might argue, for example, that all reasonable people would agree that parents are responsible to provide for their children or that our elders deserve respect and care. (And if people disagree, they thereby prove *themselves* unreasonable. Circular arguments have certain advantages.)[62] Wesley here used reason, not as a tool or processor, but as a set of conclusions derived from this process. These conclusions, he believed, were firmly established and would be agreed to by all reasonable persons. In reality, among this list are many things that appear to reflect Wesley's cultural assumptions and would not be agreed on in all cultures or times. It is clear that these claims are based on particular experiences of his time and culture and not simply on reason alone. We will return to this point after looking at the extent and limits of reason that are implied in Wesley's definition of reason as a tool or capacity for understanding.

The Extent and Limits of Reason

We have seen that Wesley recognized clear limits to the work of reason. Reason does not have independent, unmediated access to divine knowledge or to any knowledge, for that matter. It simply processes and works from information received from other sources. What can this limited reason do? What is its extent?[63]

If Wesley was a pessimist about the limits of reason alone, he was an optimist about the possibilities of reason in good company. When reason is accompanied by the data of the ordinary senses, the spiritual senses, and particularly the revelation of Scripture, it helps not only in the tasks of daily life, but also in religion, and even in matters of Christian faith. Reason alone can accomplish very little; reason in good company can do many things.

In our daily life, reason has tremendous practical, instrumental value. Wesley asks, "Who can deny that it can do much, very much in the affairs of common life?"[64] Basic survival depends on reason. Human reason, moving from the data of everyday experience, gives us sufficient knowledge to carry on our work and to take care of our ordinary needs.[65] Reason helps us to know and fulfill our duties. "It can direct servants how to perform the various works wherein they are employed. . . . It can direct the husbandman at what time and in what manner to cultivate his ground. . . . It can direct the mariner to steer his course over the bosom of the great deep."[66] Whether we are servants, artists, parents, or political leaders, reason is essential. All of the arts, sciences, and other branches of human knowledge depend on reason. So, reason, working with the data derived from ordinary experience, can get us a long way.

We would probably all agree, Wesley noted, that reason helps in daily life, but how does it help in religion? In Wesley's words, "What can it do in the things of God?"[67] Reasons helps with both "the foundation" and "the superstructure" of religion.[68] As we have seen, reason alone does not give us direct access to knowledge about God. But through reason reflecting on Scripture, we can know many things about God and the moral law. We can know about the coming of Christ and his sacrificial death. We can understand more about God's will in history. We can discern the law given to us in Scripture. Scripture is always the primary resource and norm for religious knowledge, but reason is always necessary to understand and communicate it.

Another source of human knowledge of God is the spiritual senses. Through the eyes of our spiritual senses, opened for the faithful by the Holy Spirit, we can sense for ourselves, in a limited way, something of the eternal realm. Reason, in partnership revelation, helps in all of these matters. In fact, without reason, we could not understand revelation (whether from creation, Scripture, or the spiritual senses). Without the tool of reason, humans would be unable to comprehend doctrine, to preach the gospel, to make sense of the creeds, or to think about theology.[69] Reason reflecting on Scripture and other sources can get us a long way, but reason alone yields nothing.

What knowledge can we have without the immediate revelation of Scripture or of our spiritual senses? Can the tool of reason, reflecting on God's revelation in creation, lead us to any knowledge of religion? Wesley believed that humans, without the aid of Scripture or faith, could know some basic things about God and morality. Because of our shared human capacity for reason, our common experience of God's revelation in creation, and the additional gift of prevenient grace, all human beings, even without faith in Christ or access to Scripture, can know a few general things about morality and about God's existence and attributes.[70] Reason is not the source of this knowledge but a shared capacity or tool that works with our experience.

How do we come to know these things? Creation itself reflects God's nature.[71] Wesley wrote that "nature is the art of God."[72] What can we know about God from the evidence of creation? He insisted that "proofs of a wise, a good and a powerful Being are deducible from everything around us. . . . The world around us is a mighty volume wherewith God hath declared himself."[73] We can know that God rewards and judges.[74] We can know that God works providentially in history (though we know "amazingly little of the particulars").[75] In ways that seem incredibly naive to most of us, Wesley asserted that we can know that God exists and is eternal, wise, good, merciful, omnipresent, and omnipotent.[76] Wesley wrote, "Some great truths, as the being and attributes of God, and the difference between moral good and evil were known, in some measure, to the heathen world, the traces of these are found in all nations."[77]

But even though the "heathen" may know that God *has* these characteristics, they cannot fully *understand* the divine characteristics. Moreover, without additional revelation, humans cannot know the specifics about God's nature and God's saving activity in the world. And, most important, without additional revelation and grace, humans can know that God exists, but cannot *know* God. Wesley compared our knowledge of God to the knowledge of a person. "As we know there is an emperor of China, whom yet we do not know; so we knew there was a King of all the earth, but yet we knew Him not. Indeed we could not by any of our natural faculties."[78] We may know *that* God exists and yet know very little about God, much less know God for ourselves.

So, reason reflecting on creation and experience may get us *part* of the way, but it never gets us to the *heart* of religion; it does not get us the most crucial things in matters of faith. And because even our knowledge of creation and human life is limited, we should not be surprised that it does not yield much religious knowledge. Wesley writes, "O how little do we know even concerning ourselves! What then can we expect to know concerning the whole creation of God."[79] And because we know so little about creation, we cannot expect to know much about God.[80]

Reason reflecting on creation can also lead to rudimentary moral knowledge.[81] Even without Scripture, conscience allows humans to know basic moral laws. God gave humans the moral law "not wrote indeed upon tables of stone, or any corruptible substance, but engraven on his heart by the finger of God, wrote in the inmost spirit both of men and of angels."[82] When Wesley says that these laws are "engraven" on our hearts, it sounds as if he is referring to moral knowledge as an innate idea. You might ask, "But didn't he clearly reject innate ideas in other passages?" Yes, he did. And even in this very sermon, Wesley went on to insist that because of human sin in the fall, the human "well-nigh effaced [the law] out of his heart."[83] But how do we know the law if it has been "effaced" from our hearts? The law revealed in Scripture is one source of moral knowledge after the fall. In addition, moral knowledge is available through our moral sense or conscience, which is "not natural; but a supernatural gift of God, above all his natural endowments." It is "a branch of that supernatural gift of God which we usually style 'preventing grace.'"[84]

Wesley's understanding of the gift of conscience was finally empirical in the sense that once this capacity is given by God, it becomes a source for data. Human moral knowledge is still ultimately derived from the senses. Just as reason can draw on data received from physical senses, so also can it work from the data from the moral sense or conscience.[85] As humans, regardless of their religion, use reason to reflect on the data provided by human conscience, they are able to know the basic outlines of morality and the most fundamental social and familial responsibilities. Wesley wrote, "Whether this is natural or superadded by the grace of God, it is found, at least in some small degree, in every child of man. Something of this is found in every human heart, passing sentence concerning good and evil."[86]

Finally, while reason's understanding of God, the moral law, and our true human nature is limited, we can know something about our nature with certainty. Through the gift of prevenient grace, we can know that we are sinners under God's judgment. Because we recognize our sin and the corruption of our capacities (including our reason and our senses), we see that our knowledge is always limited. Though reason, prompted by prevenient grace and reflecting on creation, can get us much knowledge (even religious and moral knowledge), it has clear limits. Although it can help us know what we need to survive in the world and even to have the most rudimentary knowledge of God and morality, it cannot teach us what is most important about God and the Christian life.

What specifically *are* reason's limits? As we saw above, reason, reflecting on creation, can lead to a little knowledge about God but not to detailed knowledge. We cannot get a fully developed theology or particular doctrines. For example, humans cannot come to any knowledge about the Trinity through merely reflecting on creation.[87] Only by drawing on the sources of Scripture and tradition can human reason make sense of the Trinity. (Of course, we do not *fully* understand the Trinity even *with* the help of Scripture and tradition.) Through reason reflecting on creation, we cannot understand the pillars of classical Christian theology or many specific details about morality. We cannot come to a direct knowledge of or a personal relationship with God.

Reason also fails to produce the three primary Christian virtues: faith, hope, and love. Though faith is consistent with reason, it is not produced by reason. Faith is, instead, "a divine evidence, bringing a full conviction of an invisible eternal world." Though humans may have a faint impression of the eternal world through reason, this impression is not actually faith. Wesley wrote, "It is true there was a kind of shadowy persuasion of this, even among the wiser heathens. . . ."[88] But "shadowy persuasions" are not conviction; they are not true faith.

Because the Christian hope in God and the future depends ultimately on faith and because reason cannot summon faith, it cannot now summon hope. And because reason does not lead to faith or hope, neither can it lead to the love of God. And without loving God, humans cannot genuinely love their neighbors. Reason may be able to know something about love, but it cannot produce love. Wesley wrote, "Cold reason . . . can draw us a fine picture of love; but this is only a painted fire! And farther than this reason cannot go."[89]

As if this weren't enough, Wesley insisted that reason has further limits. Without genuine love of God and neighbor, true virtue is impossible. And without virtue, faith, hope, and love, reason cannot produce true happiness. So, even though reason, reflecting on creation and ordinary experience, can lead to some knowledge about religion, it can never bring us to the heart of religion. Furthermore, even once we *have* faith, reason is still limited. The faithful Christian, using reason to reflect on the knowledge gleaned from Scripture and other sources, still cannot know everything. Though humans have an insatiable desire for knowledge, the desire cannot be fulfilled until the end of time. Reason is limited, even when working with the data from Scripture and the spiritual senses. It can never match our insatiable desire for knowledge. Only in eternity may full knowledge be possible.[90]

Reason is limited by several factors. As we have seen, it is limited by its nature and function as a tool. Solitary reason is never a source of knowledge, only a processor of knowledge. It is also tainted by human sin. Like many other Anglicans, Wesley believed that reason after the fall is largely intact. But like the Continental reformers and some Anglicans, Wesley also insisted on the pervasive taint that comes with original sin. We may still have our reason after the fall, but it is subject to distortion and deceit. Wesley wrote,

> Let a musician be ever so skillful, he will make but poor music if his instrument be out of tune. From a disordered brain (such as is, more or less, that of every child of man) there will necessarily arise confusedness of apprehension, showing itself in a thousand instances; false judgment, the natural result thereof; and wrong inferences; and from these innumerable mistakes will follow, in spite of all the caution we can use.[91]

Sinful humans may be led astray, then, by their reason. Reason can lead to false conclusions, even among Christians. Consequently, Wesley's private letters of counsel often included cautions about reason. "Idle," "vain," or "unprofitable" reasoning can lead Christians away from faith.[92] Wesley even urged some to "beware of" or "watch against" "evil reasoning" or "the reasoning devil."[93] Advising one Christian woman to look after the spiritual welfare of another, Wesley wrote, "If possible, guard her against evil reasoning; that she may never let go her simplicity."[94] Because reason can be more easily distorted in a time of doubt or spiritual crisis, Wesley advised people in such circumstances not to be overly dependent on reason, but to trust as a little child on God's goodness and love.[95] Ultimately, the remedy to evil reasoning or to reason's limits was not reliance on external authorities or texts but simple reliance on God.

The limits of reason may spring partially from sin and the fall, but this limit has another source as well. Human reason is limited for a divine reason. The limits of reason are not all bad; they have a holy purpose. Wesley believed that the limitation of human reason is established by God as a remedy or a curb to human pride. Our basic ignorance should lead to humility and resignation, by which we are drawn toward faith and reliance on God.[96] And, ironically, this faithful reliance on God, out of the weakness and limitation of knowledge, leads to greater knowledge and power. It is through trust in God that our spiritual senses are opened so that we see and know more of God. Through that infusion of divine love, prompted by limitation and subsequent trust in God, new power and knowledge are given. Our ignorance has a therapeutic purpose, driving us to trust in God and thereby leading us to greater knowledge.

We may conclude then that reason had clear limits for Wesley. Without the revelation of Scripture and without faith, it cannot produce the things most essential to Christian life. Reason has limits even for Christians. It is subject to error and can never, this side of eternity, reach full knowledge of the spiritual realm. Yet, for all these limits, reason is still necessary, not only to survive and to fulfill our basic obligations, but also to read Scripture, to preach the faith, to teach doctrine, and to live a righteous life.

Reason in a "Post-Rational" World

When Wesley insisted that reason was necessary for religion, he was working with a very precise eighteenth-century definition of reason and its tasks. As we have seen, Wesley and other empiricists denied that reason is an independent source of knowledge and claimed, instead, that reason is a capacity of the human mind that processes data received from experience. Reason reflecting on human experiences (including our experiences of God's revelation) is a necessary part of all of life, including faith. Reason helps understand and work with Scripture, experience, and tradition. Reason confirms what we learn from these other sources. In the company of these other sources, reason can do many things; but reason alone is useless.

Like the pick ax without the coal mine, it yields nothing. Wesley crafted his model of reason out of the context of his times. He sought to find a middle way between those who valued reason too much and others who valued reason too little. He tried to negotiate his own middle ground in the debate between the Aristotelians and the Platonists. Wesley's reflections on reason are deeply tied to the context of these debates in eighteenth-century England. We also see the evidence of this cultural connection when Wesley moves from talking of reason as a tool to focus on reason as providing obvious conclusions to all reasonable persons. Living in such a different culture from Wesley and having experiences of many diverse cultures, we are more hesitant than he was to claim too much about the settled conclusions of all reasonable people.

How can a model tied so closely to eighteenth-century England speak to us in the late twentieth century? It would be easy to dismiss Wesley's understanding of reason as culturally bound and irrelevant for our context. And why shouldn't we dismiss it? Even though Wesley's work forms United Methodist theology and is a part of our standards of doctrine, we are not bound by literal allegiance to *all* aspects of Wesley's thought. Just because *he* defined reason in this way does not mean *we* must follow suit. His definitions of reason rely finally not on a higher authority, such as Scripture, but on the philosophical discussions of his own context. If we are not strictly bound by his eighteenth-century model of reason, does it have anything to say to our time? The following pages describe the place of reason in *our* theological context and suggest what Wesley might offer to us.

Like Wesley, we too are confronted by those who "despise and vilify" reason and others who "extol" it "to the skies." Surely our century has produced reason's most fervent admirers and its most unrelenting critics. Modernist theology, widespread in the early part of our century, buttressed the Enlightenment's confidence in reason with heroic accounts of its role in scientific innovation and democratic reform. The new models of evolutionary social progress fueled optimism about the potential of human reason and achievement, but the cleft between modernism's day and ours is deep. Our two worlds are separated by decades of destruction, by two world wars and dozens of guerrilla conflicts, by the annihilation of six million Jews and the starvation of millions of others, by the rise and fall of mid-century fascism in Germany and the emergence of a new fascism in

Bosnia, by the rise and fall of communist repression and the violent extension of the worst forms of capitalism. Any evidence of human evolution appears to be counterbalanced by the horrifying evidence of our devolution. Advances in medicine, food production, and communication are matched by the brutality made possible by other technologies. If reason can be credited for scientific technologies of healing, it can surely be blamed for technologies of destruction.

These brutal facts have brought reason under fire. Modern confidence in reason has been replaced by a "postmodern" suspicion. Many philosophers and theologians not only blame reason for its part in the violence of our century, but also question the very existence of any unembedded or pure human reason. They claim that all human reason is fully shaped (and misshapen) by culture. There is no one common human rationality, but only different, culturally specific systems of rationality. Though postmodernists begin from a shared rejection of common reason or experience, they move in different directions, responding to this shared diagnosis with two contrasting remedies. One branch, the "postmodern traditionalists," calls for our immersion in our own culturally specific tradition of rationality. Given the limits of human reason, true conversation and understanding are possible only within a specific tradition.

On the other side, "postmodern radicals" begin from similar assumptions about the relativity of human reason as well as the relativity of larger traditions of rationality, but move in a very different direction. They are highly suspicious of the dominant traditions of rationality that they criticize for reflecting and promoting the interests of the powerful. Models of reason are formed by the interests of the powerful and become a tool to further the interests of the powerful. Consequently, the remedy to the relative nature of human reason and knowledge is not immersion in one tradition, but comprehensive interaction with many traditions, so that we at least might realize the limits of our own perspective and perhaps find resources for new approaches. Though they end up in very different places, both groups of postmodernists reject the idea of any pure, unencumbered reason or common human experience.

These are not reason's only detractors. We also find more familiar traditional Protestant critics who emphasize the full corruption of human reason by sin and the fall. Because reason is so corrupt, humans must rely completely on revelation from without, primarily from Scripture. These critics are joined by other detractors of reason,

101

who focus not so much on Scripture but on some aspect of experience. Among some in holiness and especially in charismatic traditions, the immediate experience of the Spirit is primary. And in other segments of popular culture (Christian and secular), we find a strong reliance on a different aspect of experience—the subjective experience of the individual or a defined community of individuals. Subjective experience becomes the ultimate authority and norm, trumping other authorities. For these experience-centered groups, reason is often suspect; it can be seen as a cold, technical refusal of the immediacy of experience.

If the tide of our century has moved away from reliance on reason, we can still spot some moving against this tide, for reason still has its admirers. Though tempered by the brutalities of our century, many Christians still look to reason as a primary source for faith and theology. Certainly, a generation ago, thinkers like Martin Luther King, Jr., and Georgia Harkness were highly confident about the power of human reason to know about God and moral truth. And in our decade, many natural law thinkers (Catholic *and* Protestant) and process theologians, for example, still share great confidence in reason's powers to discern not only the relative truths of the culture, but also the Truths that cut across or transcend cultures and generations. Certainly, for many in our churches, postmodernity's suspicion of reason is not widespread. Many people in our churches maintain a modern and even a premodern confidence in human reason. How complex is the ecclesial theologian's task!

Faced with this array of critics and defenders of reason, can we find anything of help in Wesley? Is he a fruitful resource for contemporary discourse? In spite of the huge differences in the assumptions about reason in Wesley's time and ours, I find several factors in Wesley's understanding and use of reason that are congenial to today's discussions. I also find aspects of Wesley's thought that *challenge* contemporary discussion and are challenged *by* contemporary discussion.

How is Wesley's model congenial to our context? Given the postmodern suspicion of reason and the liberal emphasis on experience, Wesley's Aristotelian empiricist model, with its limited role for reason, is less foreign than a Platonic model that affirms innate ideas or unquestionable first principles. Wesley would probably not be an advocate of abstract absolute truth claims, especially if such claims are made in ways that are similar to, or rooted in, Platonic concepts.

Beyond his rejection of innate ideas and his limited focus on reason as a tool rather than as a source for knowledge, what other aspects of Wesley's Aristotelian model are particularly familiar? First, Wesley and many in our day share an appeal to concrete experience as a ground of theology. Wesley may be more confident about our common experience than some postmodernists, but they do share an appeal to particular experience. Second, both Wesley and many contemporary theologians understand reason's work as piecemeal, pragmatic, and limited. Reason reflects on multiple sources from experience and leads us to sufficient knowledge to get along in the world. Third, like Wesley, many contemporary theologians insist that reason is not separated from the body or disembodied. Reason is, instead, fully embodied. It works with and through the bodily experience of the senses. Fourth, Wesley's model of reason, like many contemporary understandings, does not pit reason against emotion. Reason is not anti-emotional. In fact, reason and the affections are closely linked. Ultimately, for Wesley, the highest knowledge comes when we live in love. Fifth, many recent thinkers would find the democratic or egalitarian aspects of Wesley's view of reason congenial. Because all have the capacities for sensing the environment, for processing the data through reason, and for experiencing God's grace, Wesley's model has an egalitarian slant.

Finally, for Wesley, reason's work is not a self-enclosed, individual task. Reason's extent depends on the abundant resources of the environment, including discourse with other people and traditions. Reason always works in conversation. Thus, Christian "conference" is necessary to theological reasoning. This Wesleyan point is especially important in the current debates around postmodernity. Reason works in conversation not only to help us discern the truth but also to show us the limitations of our facile claims about the truth. When conversation is open to many perspectives, we are less likely to make overly broad claims (as Wesley did!) based in our own culture about what all "reasonable people" would accept. At the same time, conference allows us greater confidence in those claims that we do arrive at together. This Wesleyan model of reason as a tool that can reflect on experience is less grand than some modern claims about reason, but it is also more substantial than some postmodern suspicion of reason.

There are, however, obvious differences between Wesley and our postmodern context. As we have seen, Wesley was more optimistic than some postmodernists about our shared human capacity for reason that, when accompanied by experience, could come to clear truth. He was confident about what "all rational people" could agree on. And perhaps this is the focus of our corrective to Wesley. Because we have greater exposure to many different, contrasting cultures, it is difficult for us to be as confident as Wesley was about what "all rational people" ought to believe. In a more homogenous culture, it is easier to assume that one's *own* reason is universal reason. So, Wesleyans today add a critical corrective to Mr. Wesley, keeping an eye on the deep, genuine differences that exist across human cultures. Contemporary Wesleyans can offer another critical corrective. Though Wesley was highly aware of the reality of sin and human self-interest, he did not exhibit a high level of sensitivity, as many in our century do, to the use and misuse of reason by those in power to further their own interests. Thus, contemporary Wesleyans can offer a critical corrective, being more suspicious about claims concerning "what all rational people believe," and about the place of human power in shaping our ideas of what is rational. These critical perspectives from the contemporary debate can be fruitful for Wesleyans. We can revise Wesley's model given the new experiences and insights of our context. But how does Wesley revise our models? How does he correct us?

Certainly Wesley, along with many others, contradicts the postmodern denial of common human experience. Many postmodernists tend to dismiss claims for common experience as culturally naive. And, as I suggested above, perhaps these critics are partly right. Perhaps some aspects of Wesley's argument, such as his claims about what "all rational people believe" do not account for the genuine differences across cultures. But Wesley's appeal to common human experience, reason, or other capacities is not ultimately based in cultural or sociological investigation. In the end, these claims are theological. For Wesley, the ground of our common experiences and capacities (including reason) is God. Here Wesley is in distinct continuity with his Anglican heritage,[97] as chapter one has shown. Through God's grace (shown in creation, restoration, transforming presence, etc.), we have common capacities and experience. His insistence on common human experience and reason is not simply an empirical claim that is grounded in previous cultural observation and that can therefore be disproved by new cultural observation. It is a faith claim, a faith in continuity of experience with all the faithful who have preceded. It is a theological claim. Wesley's theology reminds Christians that even if the anthropological or cultural data points to extreme differences in human experience, we ground claims about our common experience in God's creating and restoring grace. And if one *does* believe that we share common nature and capacities through God's creation, restoration, and continuing presence, then that shared nature is a legitimate ground for further moral and theological claims. It provides a foundation for moral claims that many postmodernists have forgone. It is a realist or naturalist claim about shared human reason and experience that is grounded theologically as much as it is in anthropological evidence.

Though a primary block for many postmodernists is Wesley's confidence in reason, the most illuminating contribution comes not when Wesley speaks of the extent of reason, but when he focuses on its limits. Within postmodernity, the denial of modern confidence in reason has prompted crisis and despair. The loss of confidence in reason, in human access to Truth, can lead to resignation. Postmodernists have offered alternate remedies for this problem. According to the "radical postmodernists" on the left, we should respond to the limits of our own traditions of rationality by turning to the voices of people from other traditions of rationality. For the "traditionalist postmodernists" on the right, we respond to the limitation of our reason by relying on the language of our own tradition. Though Wesley valued Christian conference, was open to the hearing of other perspectives, and clearly called for faithfulness to our traditions, these were not the primary remedies when he came upon reason's limits in pastoral situations.

What did Wesley do when he ran into the limits of human reason? As was noted above, when he saw that human reasoning was leading some astray, he cautioned them to turn from "evil" or "idle" reasoning to a simple trust in God. In these pastoral situations, he did not normally say "rely on your pastor," "turn to the first five centuries," "trust in the creeds," or even "turn to Scripture." Wesley's remedy was to turn to God in childlike trust. In coming up against the limits of reason, we are driven to God. But, ironically, this remedy does not end with simple resignation to our limited knowledge and reason. Trusting in God when our reason is limited is not the end of reason and knowledge, but the beginning. Out of our limits, through the power of God's grace, our spiritual senses are opened and we have not less knowledge but more. The limits are themselves therapeutic; they are a means of divine grace, driving us toward God and ultimately toward greater spiritual knowledge. Reason's limits lead not to despair, or to a return to a fixed tradition, or to the hearing of many voices from different cultures. Reason's limits can lead to trust in God, becoming not an occasion for despair but a means of grace.

This model offers us a very different alternative to the two common options of postmodernity. As we face postmodern claims about the limits of reason, we have not only the options of the postmodern traditionalists and radicals, but also the option offered by Wesley in these pastoral situations. Perhaps the limits of reason are not occasions for despair or for over-reliance on fixed traditions or other finite human voices, but for a recognition of our limits and a trust in the transforming presence and power of God's grace. This presence transcends and goes beyond human knowledge while making human knowledge possible. It is a dynamic, present transcendence. It is in this grace that the church can discern again the voice of God.

Chapter Five

The Enriching Role of Experience

Randy L. Maddox

"I'm tired of having my interpretations of Scripture dismissed simply because they aren't orthodox. Everyone interprets Scripture from his or her experience, study and reason. Are we supposed to turn off our minds and let traditionalists think for us?"[1]

It would be hard to find a more representative glimpse of the current debate over the Quadrilateral among United Methodists than this excerpt from a recent letter to the editor of the *United Methodist Reporter*. It illustrates that the lines in the debate typically find their most forceful expression in off-the-cuff remarks rather than in careful programmatic presentations. It captures the level of passion permeating the debate. It reflects the tendency of the opposing parties to frame the debate in terms of a stark dichotomy: *either* we think for ourselves by relying on our individual experience and reason, *or* we submit ourselves to tradition. And it uses the words "reason" and "experience" as if their meanings are self-evident.

There is nothing wrong with passionate involvement in a debate when one is convinced that vital truths are at stake. However, it is important in these situations to insure that our passion does not override honest consideration of alternative views. Such evaluation could result in clarifications that facilitate constructive progress in the discussion. With this potential in view, I want to offer some clarifications about the nature of experience and the various possible roles that experience might play in theological reflection, drawing on the example of John Wesley's appeals to experience. Reflection on this example should be informative for the present United Methodist debate, since Wesley's emphasis on experience was formative of our interest in this topic. I will begin by using it to challenge the apparent assumption of many participants in this debate that the meaning of "experience" is clear, or unambiguous.

Alternative Conceptions of Experience

Consider the following situation: A patient of a group medical practice is slated for surgery and insists on "the benefit of experience" in the operation. A puzzled nurse responds "Well, if you insist, but most of our patients consider it a benefit to have anesthesia so that they do *not* experience the operation!" The patient retorts rather curtly, "I did not mean that I want to feel the operation, but that I want a physician with experience in this procedure." "In that case," the helpful nurse replies, "you will want Dr. White. She has not performed the surgery before, but she has had it herself, so she will understand what you are going through!"

As this hypothetical case shows, "experience" can be a very ambiguous term. There is no reason to assume that theological discussions escape this ambiguity. On the contrary, it is quite likely that some of the confrontations over using experience in making doctrinal decisions result from the opponents having in mind different conceptions of experience. This means that an initial step in building greater agreement on the legitimate contribution of experience to Christian life and teaching would be to clarify the major alternative conceptions of this ambiguous entity.[2] Sorting out the three conceptions that create the humorous miscues in our hypothetical case is a good place to begin.

Conscious Awareness of Being Affected by an Event or Action

The first miscue in the conversation of our hypothetical patient and nurse arose when the nurse assumed that the patient's request for "experience" was a request to remain conscious so that he could be aware of the subjective effect of the operation upon him. This use of "experience" to denote consciously undergoing an event or action is a common one. It can be clearly seen in Wesley's question "Art thou acquainted with the leading of [God's] Spirit, not by notion only, but by living experience?"[3] As the question illustrates, this use often emphasizes the subjective dimension of being affected in direct contrast with a merely objective or abstract consideration of the source of the affect.

The Oxford English Dictionary points out that this use of "experience" takes on particular prominence in religious traditions that highlight the need for a "felt" personal relationship with God.[4] Since Methodism is the specific example cited, it is not surprising that instances with this stress abound in Wesley. One of the clearest cases is a letter where he insists that even if a man is morally upright and attends all the proper religious ordinances, "He is not to think well of his own state till he experiences something within himself which he has not yet experienced . . . a sure trust and confidence in God . . . the love of God shed abroad in his heart."[5]

Sympathetic Understanding Derived from Similar Subjective Experience

The second miscue in our hypothetical case came as the nurse tried switching to a closely related meaning of "experience." The basic concern of this meaning is still with the subjective dimension of undergoing an event or action, but the focus shifts from the occasion of oneself being affected to the insight gained through this occasion that enables us to sympathize with others who undergo similar events or actions. While this second meaning is less common in culture at large, and in Wesley, a good example of it can be found in his prefatory comments to his edition of Thomas à Kempis's classic book *The Imitation of Christ*:

> . . . the great practical truths of religion, the mysteries of the inward kingdom of God, cannot be fully discerned, but by those readers who have read the same things in their own souls. These cannot be clearly known, but by those who derive their knowledge, "not from commentaries, but experience;" who, by living the life of Christ, by treading in his steps, and suffering the will of God to rule in them as it did in Him, have attained to what the heart of a natural man cannot conceive . . . inward, practical, experimental, feeling knowledge.[6]

Practical Skill Developed through Repeated Performance

The patient's intended meaning of "experience," which our nurse kept missing, related not to any subjective affect on the person undergoing an operation but to the practical skill developed by the physician performing the operation. This is the sense in which we speak of "experienced" professionals and artisans. We typically are trying to designate persons who have become adept at their trade, not by book instruction alone, but by long practice under a variety of circumstances. This connotation is suggested in Wesley's praise for those Methodist society members who have "more skill or more experience" with visiting the sick, and those preachers who are "deeply experienced in the work of God, accustomed to train up souls in [God's] way."[7]

Practical/Moral Wisdom Derived from Life-long Learning

As we move beyond the senses of "experience" suggested in my opening example, in search of other senses evident in Wesley's writings, the first addition to note is closely related to the sense just treated. Just as we can develop skill in a craft or trade by long-term practice, it has long been recognized that we also can develop wisdom about the "art of living" through the challenges and opportunities encountered over the course of our lives. This wisdom typically integrates practical insights with moral sensitivities, which explains why Wesley stressed that those chosen for leadership roles in the church should have the benefits of the experience that comes with age.[8] Of course, Wesley recognized that this is not an automatic process. For wisdom to grow with age, we must remain sensitive and willing to learn, particularly to learn from our mistakes. This sensitivity is reflected in Wesley's hope—expressed when the congregation at the Foundery in London was evidencing a revitalization after over two decades of stagnation—that he and his brother Charles would not quench the Spirit here this time, as they had before, because they had "learned experience by the things we have suffered."[9]

Practical Test or Trial as Means of Determining Truth

Against the backdrop of the recognition that living through the practical trials of life can be a source of moral/spiritual wisdom, it is easier to understand another use of "experience" in Wesley that sounds quite odd to modern ears. This use equates "experience" with the action of using practical tests or trial-and-error to determine truth. It was a common use in English prior to Wesley, as reflected in Wycliffe's 1388 translation of Genesis 42:15 (where Joseph announces that he is going to put his brothers to a test) as "Now I shall take experience of you."[10]

While it still found resonance in Wesley, this use of "experience" was well on the road to becoming obsolete.[11] A good way to capture its distance from present assumptions is to note Wesley's complaint against the emerging professionalization of medicine in his day. He faulted them with "setting experience aside" and building medical research instead on hypotheses.[12] By this he was protesting their tendency to discount traditional folk cures that had been discovered through centuries of trial-and-error, accepting only those cures whose effectiveness could be explained by modern scientific methods. While Wesley appreciated the prominent role of empirical observation in modern science, he questioned the assumption that reliable insights into truth emerge *only* in professional environments where research is focused on testing prespecified hypotheses. He was convinced that we should continue to value the way that truth is discovered through the accidents of life and ordinary trial-and-error, even in a field like medicine.[13]

This conviction is reflected in Wesley's *Journal* by his frequent inclusion of instances of discerning truth through ordinary events or trial-and-error. One quaint example is his account of how experience delivered him from his fear of camping out when circumstances required him to sleep outdoors; the test proved that it was not detrimental to his health.[14] A more important example is his argument that experience demonstrates that the Lord's Supper is a "converting ordinance," since many of his followers had found in practice that their conversion could be traced back to when they overcame the traditional inhibitions and approached the Table.[15] This example should alert us that many of his appeals to experience in relation to doctrinal disputes involve seeking truth through such practical testing.

Observation of Facts or Events as a Source of Knowledge

The main reason that many of Wesley's peers did not join him in championing a continuing role for the type of practical testing depended on in earlier times for determining truth was that they were searching for a method that would provide greater certainty. They lived in the period after the medieval assumption that all truth was firmly established and reliably conveyed in tradition had been challenged and abandoned. While early Renaissance thinkers had optimistically predicted that this change would spawn a tolerance of conflicting viewpoints in Western culture, the actual result was armed conflict between competing orthodoxies in both the religious and the political fields. In desperation, early Enlightenment thinkers groped for a way to resolve the intellectual differences between the competing parties, so that the fighting could stop. The most influential figures decided that the only hope lay in finding a method of

111

determining truth that could be publicly verified and provided absolute certainty.[16]

The irony of this noble Enlightenment venture is that philosophers ended up fighting among themselves about where the reliable means to certainty could be found—was it in the logical purity of reason or the objective facticity of empirical observation? The latter option came to dominate British and North American colonial thought in the eighteenth century and stamped an enduring empiricist cast on modern Western culture. The word "experience" took on a distinctive meaning under this empiricist cast. It now denoted verifiable *observation* of present facts and events (with experiments aimed more at enhancing the possibility of observation than at trial-and-error testing), or the knowledge gained from such observation.

Wesley developed a strong commitment to formal Enlightenment empiricism through his Oxford education.[17] More important, he shared the larger culture's tendency to associate empiricism with "common sense." Thus, when a detractor of Methodism asked mockingly whether Wesley had gotten his knowledge of the possibility of deliverance from sin by some special inspiration, he retorted sharply, "No; but by common sense. I know it by the evidence of my own eyes and ears. I have seen a considerable part of it; and I have abundant testimony, such as excludes all possible doubt, for what I have not seen."[18] This popularized empiricism is evident in a significant percentage of Wesley's uses of "experience," including many instances invoking it in support of theological claims. He often emphasizes that the evidence he has in mind is publicly verifiable by specifying "daily experience" as demonstrating claims such as the need of newly converted persons for further spiritual transformation, since they are not instantaneously freed from the "seeds" of unholy attitudes and desires.[19]

The Mediated Nature of Human Experience

The six conceptions of experience just surveyed likely cover the range that Wesley would have been able to distinguish, if pressed to do so, because they were all current in his day. Dictionaries indicate that the first and last conceptions, in particular, remain in common use. However, the careful observer will sense that a unique twist is typically given to these two conceptions today. This twist is hinted at in the quote that opened this chapter, with its emphasis on *each individual's* experience. By contrast, we just noted Wesley's emphasis on the public verifiability of empirical observation, and he was characteristically skeptical of unusual (i.e., highly individual) accounts of the subjective affect of encounter with God.[20] Behind this difference in emphasis lies our cultural confrontation with the mediated nature of human experience, which was just beginning in philosophical circles in Wesley's latter years.

This confrontation can be best understood by comparing it with the optimism of the Enlightenment empiricists. We saw above that their initial hope was to locate a method that could generate absolutely certain knowledge. Most of them soon conceded, under rationalist critique, that knowledge based on inductive observation of particulars would always fall short of logical certainty. However, they still optimistically maintained that this knowledge was *objective* (revealing things as they truly are) and *categorical* (true for all persons, cultures, and times). This confidence was based on their assumption that the mind was a purely receptive instrument in the knowing process, contributing nothing of its own to an individual's knowledge.

Through the eighteenth century it became increasingly hard to overlook the point that this empiricist assumption did not square with the reality that persons of goodwill and mental competence often disagree in their observational reports of the same event or "fact." While there have been various attempts to get around it, the conclusion that this reality has forced upon most philosophers is that our minds contribute actively to observation (and other types of "experience"). As Immanuel Kant formulated it in an influential thesis: all human experience is *interpreted* experience, because it is *mediated* through our preexisting intellectual concepts.

The potential skeptical implications of this thesis were offset for Kant himself by focusing on interpretive concepts that he believed were universally shared and invariant, like space and time. Even before Einstein could nuance this assumption, most of Western culture was being influenced by sociology and psychology to focus instead on the cultural and individual ways that our interpretations of experience vary. The cumulative result of this is the current tendency, at least in popular culture, to reduce experience to mere "perspective." Few any longer assume that experience provides knowledge that is objective and categorical. Instead, experience is assumed to provide simply my perspective (either as a typical white, middle-aged, middle-class, North American male; or as a unique individual) on what I take to be reality! The obvious questions about (1) whether my perspective corresponds in any way to how things truly are, and (2) what claim it has against other varying perspectives, are at the heart of the vigorous debates going on in late twentieth-century Western culture.[21]

The insistence on honoring each individual's experience in the quotation with which this chapter began reflects that these questions are also central to current United Methodist debate over theological method. It might appear that Wesley has little to offer in dealing with such questions, since he predated their broad cultural emergence. But if we look closely, we can see his dawning awareness of the mediated nature of human experience, and of the challenges it would entail.

One of the early glimmers of this awareness is in Wesley's sermonic distillation of his major treatise on *The Doctrine of Original Sin*. The original treatise could serve as a showcase of the Enlightenment optimism within which he was trained. The central argument was ostensibly an objective empirical survey of human behavior, past and present. It drew on Scripture, but only as a historical record. And it concluded boldly, based on the evidence cited, that the universality of sin should be obvious to "even the most careless, inaccurate observer."[22] In comparison, the sermon that distilled this treatise just two years later was more reserved. Here Wesley begins with the biblical affirmation of universal human sinfulness. He then maintains that daily experience confirms this affirmation, but he immediately adds the qualification that those who have not been regenerated by God's grace typically do not discern this confirmation![23] In this move he was conceding that empirical observation is not as immediate or publicly verifiable as his earlier treatise suggested.

To be sure, this concession does not rule out the continuing optimistic assumption that all who *have* received the benefits of regeneration discern God's truth and God's work in their lives immediately, rendering objective and categorical knowledge. If Wesley was holding on to such an assumption at this point (1759), ongoing reflection upon his spiritual journey was rapidly undercutting it. This can be illustrated by his changing evaluation of the role of Aldersgate within that journey. Aldersgate had been experientially important, but a variety of factors helped Wesley to recognize how certain instilled expectations had influenced his initial interpretation of what he experienced there. In the immediate months subsequent to his Aldersgate experience, he had a rather negative assessment of his spiritual status before that event. In the years that followed he decided that his negative perspective regarding his Christian walk prior to May 24, 1738, was unwarranted or unwise, and he was compelled to offer a revised interpretation of the role of Aldersgate in his spiritual pilgrimage.[24] In this act of revising Wesley was conceding—at least implicitly—that not even regenerate believers can avoid having their experience mediated through their preexisting expectations and conceptions.[25]

The recognition of the mediated character of human experience evident in these concessions is admittedly embryonic. Even so, Wesley showed some discernment of the temptations that highlighting this character would pose for theology. The most radical temptation has been to embrace a skeptical denial that we can know whether there is even such a thing as "reality," let alone that our interpretations fit reality. Such total skepticism, while conceivable in theory, is quite rare because it is so hard to live out in practice. Even the rigorous skeptic David Hume acknowledged that he still looked forward to supper and socializing with his friends at the end of the day (which is why Wesley dismissed Hume's skepticism with such disdain).[26]

Somewhat more common is the polar temptation to rule out any reliance upon experience in seeking truth, accepting the skeptics' assumption that its mediated character renders experience totally subjective. Wesley was confronted with such a total disqualification of experience in reaction to his emphasis on a personal experience of the witness of the Spirit. In response, he willingly allowed that some people "may fancy they experience what they do not," but he strongly rejected the suggestion that such cases demonstrate that every consideration of experience would inevitably degenerate into "enthusiasm."[27] We will see below why his response would be the same today, when the reactionary suggestion to dismiss all consideration of experience is more commonly heard in relation to theological methodology.

The most subtle, and most frequent, temptation in post-Enlightenment theology has been to invoke the perspectival nature of mediated experience as a preemptive shield against any suggestion that we submit our personal experience to broader accountability—to retort, for example, "That is only *your* perspective. I am entitled to my *own!*" This type of response easily degenerates into a situation like Wesley warned of among some Christian mystics, where one finds "as many religions as books because each makes his [or her] experience the standard of truth."[28] Wesley recognized that the fundamental problem with such situations is not that we have failed to show proper respect to some abstract orthodoxy, but that we are failing to respect one another enough to allow that a sister or brother might have a more adequate sense than our own of how to live faithfully as God's people in the world.[29] That is why he continually exhorted his Methodists about the importance of "Christian conference" in nurturing our lives of holiness and in discussions of debated theological claims central to his annual "conferences" with his preachers.[30]

One obvious application of Wesley's exhortation to confer with others would be to include *him* in our present conversations about the theological implications of accepting that all human experience is mediated. This could be particularly helpful since his response to a growing awareness of this reality stands in strong contrast with the broad current tendency to accept the reduction of experience to "individual perspective," thereby casting it into the dichotomous relationship with tradition and Scripture. If we will consider Wesley's alternative seriously, it might help us to develop an enriched conception of experience and a broader awareness of the roles of experience in Christian life.

The Varied Roles of Experience in Christian Life

Wesley's emergent recognition of the mediated nature of human knowledge did not lead him to abandon any of the conceptions of experience identified above. Rather he took this reality into account in the way that he selectively utilized these conceptions within the roles that he discerned experience playing in Christian life. To appreciate his moves we will need to look beyond our focal issue of the contribution of experience to doctrinal decisions. This is only one of the roles that Wesley attributed to experience. Identifying the other roles that he discerned, and noting how he correlated certain conceptions of experience to certain roles, will help highlight the insights that his example can offer into our focal issue.

Providing Empowerment for Christ-like Living

There is no disputing the common assertion that experience plays a prominent role in Wesley's overall theology. However, it is important to recognize that a major portion of his actual appeals to experience were not directly concerned with either formulating or testing doctrinal claims. They reflected instead his emphasis on the contribution of experience to providing the assurance that empowers us for Christ-like living. This role is captured in his frequent claim that we human beings are incapable of loving God or others until we first experience God's love for us.[31] Far from being mere rhetorical flourish, this claim reflected Wesley's central assumptions about how we are able to act in moral ways—i.e., his "moral psychology."[32]

Wesley worked out his moral psychology in correlation with his empiricist commitments about human knowledge. Enlightenment empiricists denied the rationalists' suggestions that truth exists in the human intellect prior to encounter with the empirical world, or that the mind creates truth by imposing rational order upon sensory experience. They insisted instead that truth can only be acquired *responsively* through our sensory encounter with the world. Translated to the issue of moral psychology, this insistence led Wesley and many others in his day to reject the intellectualist model that dominated current Christian moral thought. This model assumed that humans naturally enact whatever they are rationally convinced is right. On this assumption, the primary task involved in moral formation is rational instruction or persuasion. While Wesley appreciated the need for such instruction, he stressed that it was inadequate by itself, because it failed to appreciate that the human will—like the human intellect—is a *responsive* instrument.

To put this point in a practical example, Wesley's emphasis entailed that no amount of rational instruction alone could enable a child to express love for others if that child had never personally experienced love from others. If we want to help such emotionally deprived children to love, we must begin by creating opportunities for them to receive love. Only as their wills are "affected" in this way will they be inclined and empowered to love in response.

This "affectional" moral psychology lies behind Wesley's emphasis on the witness of the Spirit. He viewed the witness of the Spirit as God's active personal communication of love to us. And he believed that it is only as we are inwardly affected by this witness and

117

become conscious of God's love that we are enabled to live truly Christ-like lives, loving God and others.[33]

Ironically, though this belief grew out of his application of empiricist themes to moral psychology, it also led to Wesley's major point of difference with most Enlightenment empiricists. Since they equated "experience" with observation by the natural senses, and since God does not appear directly to these senses, they typically allowed knowledge of God only on the basis of rational inference from experience. Wesley feared that such secondary inference could not provide sufficient confidence in God's love to empower our Christian lives. This led him to postulate that God created us with a set of "spiritual senses" in addition to our physical senses, so that we can be directly affected by spiritual realities like God's loving embrace.[34] This proposal involved more than adding another set of senses to the Enlightenment model. Wesley was actually rejecting the appropriateness of the Enlightenment conception of experience, with its focus on objective observation, for explaining experience's empowering affect upon Christian life. His alternative was the conception of experience as direct inward awareness.[35]

The extent to which Wesley insisted on the directness of the affect of the Spirit's witness eventually put him at odds with both classical Protestant and contemporary Anglican theology. In these realms a fear of "enthusiasm" had led to the subordination of any possible direct witness of the Spirit concerning our Christian status to the "indirect witness" of publicly discernible Christian virtues.[36] While Wesley agreed that these virtues would characterize truly Christian life, he refused to make their presence foundational to our confidence in God's loving embrace. This would be to resort again to mere inference, and possibly to works-righteousness.[37] To protect against such dangers, Wesley maintained that we directly perceive (rather than infer) that virtues like love and joy in our lives are the "fruit of the Spirit." This claim, which opponents labeled an assertion of "perceptual inspiration," became a focus of Anglican criticism of Wesley. While he was forced to offer in response several qualifications pointing to the mediated nature of experience, Wesley clung to the basic insistence that our awareness of the Spirit's work is by direct affect.[38]

In essence, Wesley was suggesting that our awareness of God's love for us is analogous to our awareness of our own affections. Before this suggestion is dismissed, I would note that it has had some recent sophisticated defenses. But I would add that if these defenses are judged convincing, Wesley's basic suggestion would need to be appropriated in a manner that takes the mediated nature of our awareness of our own affections more explicitly into account than his dawning sensitivity allowed him to do.[39]

Providing Seasoned Guidance for Our Spiritual Pilgrimage

For all of his insistence on our need for empowerment, Wesley was well aware that empowerment alone does not guarantee Christ-like living. Raw energy can destroy as easily as it enlivens; the difference lies in how wisely it is used. So, where do we look for wisdom concerning how to "put to work" that gracious empowerment that God is "working in us"? A second set of Wesley's appeals to experience highlight its role in contributing such enrichment.

The type of experience assumed in these appeals is no longer our immediate inward consciousness, because this is precisely what needs the benefit of wise guidance. Failure to seek such guidance can result in what Wesley viewed as true "enthusiasm," the confusing of mere imagination with the leading of the Spirit.[40] To guard against this we must "test the spirits." While Scripture is central to this testing, there is the parallel need to test our individual interpretation of Scripture! Extending Wesley's own moves in this direction, the way out of this circle is "conference" with other Christians. Such *corporate* testing can help us discern when our preconceptions are distorting our spiritual experience. This potential is heightened if we include in the dialogue those who have the benefit of *long-term* experience in the Christian life.

Wesley's personal benefit from corporate long-term experience is reflected in the mature pastoral advice he gave about allowing for a variety in God's ways of initiating a saving relationship in our lives (advice quite different from that which he gave immediately after Aldersgate!).[41] Given his own case, one can understand Wesley's concern that his Methodist followers benefit from dialogue with the wisdom of those past and present saints who have gained experience through the course of their spiritual pilgrimage.[42] To make this wisdom available he republished numerous spiritual biographies of saints through the ages (as models to be imitated) and gathered many of their written proverbs and manuals for spiritual formation in his fifty-volume *Christian Library*. He also cited them repeatedly. In a particularly revealing case, he invoked the seasoned wisdom of an early Christian mentor to caution those reveling in their new conversion "experience" that since they were actually still *unexperienced* they would be prone to the false assumption that this one event delivered them from all inclination to sin.[43]

One insight we can gain from Wesley in this regard is that he assumed gathering and sharing this type of experience was a central task of theology! This assumption was in keeping with earlier Christian precedent. By contrast, the historical course of Western academic theology progressively isolated materials devoted to sharing wisdom about spiritual guidance and formation from those devoted to consideration of doctrine—and denied the former truly theological status. From a Wesleyan perspective, this must be seen as one of the major weaknesses of contemporary theology, and the fledgling attempts to reclaim a model of theology that is enriched by practical wisdom should be heralded.[44]

Providing Public Evidence of Central Christian Teachings

There is no need to argue in the academy for the theological status of the next role of experience evident in Wesley's appeals. The task of providing a public defense of the central Christian claims has a long and distinguished theological career. It is occasionally suggested that Wesley shied away from this apologetic task. In reality, he simply rejected the rationalist approach that had become standard in apologetics, in favor of an Enlightenment empiricist approach. For example, he was convinced that simple observation of the order in the universe around us points to an all-wise Cosmic Designer. To demonstrate this, he compiled a multi-volume *Survey of the Wisdom of God in Creation* that summarized the current findings of scientific observation and periodically sermonized on the evidence that these findings provide for God.[45]

Defending the existence of God is only one agenda of traditional apologetics. Another was to defend the claims that Christianity makes about the nature of God and humanity that differ from claims of other religions. Wesley's commitment to an empiricist apologetic comes through in this regard as well. He frequently appeals to "daily experience" to confirm such central Christian claims as inherited depravity and the liberty of the human will from determinism.[46]

The appeal to such publicly verifiable experience is no accident, since the traditional goal of apologetics was to convince outsiders. If we broaden this goal to include enriching one's own conviction of the truth of Christian teaching, we begin to overlap with the first role of experience discussed above, because our empowerment is correlated to our conviction. This makes it significant that it is largely in cases of such overlap that Wesley emphasizes our inner awareness of God's working can confirm Christian claims, including the central claim of the definitive revelation in Scripture.[47]

Part of Wesley's motivation for turning from reason to experience in his apologetic was likely his growing conviction of reason's inability to prove any theological claim conclusively.[48] His Enlightenment rhetoric can often leave the impression that he believed experience could attain this goal. However, at other times he speaks more modestly (and in keeping with mediated experience) of such apologetic considerations simply strengthening confidence that Christian faith-claims are compatible with broadly-accepted human knowledge.

Providing Guidance in Doctrinal Decisions

We come now to the role of experience that is most focal to the present debates over theological method. This role concerns not how experience can help demonstrate the truth of established Christian teachings but the logically prior issue of how it might help the Christian community in discerning what to teach. Actually, the issue is usually how we discern what to *keep* teaching! The formulation of Christian doctrine has seldom been initiated by some official theological body and then offered to the community of believers (and when it has, it was often not "received"!). Instead, from the earliest days of the church theological claims have typically emerged out of a variety of grass-roots settings and situations, and the doctrinal task has been to discern which of these claims warranted strong refutation, which could be considered fanciful but harmless, and which should be endorsed or nurtured for broader acceptance.

Wesley's pastoral role in the Methodist movement positioned him to confront the task of doctrinal discernment often—both in justifying to the larger church why Methodists should keep teaching their distinctive claims and in assessing the unconventional currents within his movement. My co-authors show how he embraced the long-standing roles for Scripture and tradition, as well as a role for reason, in carrying out this task. He also self-consciously appealed to experience on frequent occasions as both a source and a criterion for doctrinal discernment.

Behind Wesley's appeals to experience were two theological convictions. First, he considered humanity's sensory and affective capacities to be divine endowments intended to help us perceive God's revelatory and salvific overtures. While he allowed that human fallenness has dulled and distorted these capacities, he was confident that God continued to uphold them graciously in their intended purposes.[49] Second, Wesley affirmed that God's self-revelatory activity is not limited to its normative expression in Christ, being evident as well (to the discerning) in the created order that we observe and in which we live out our practical lives.[50]

While Wesley affirmed a substantive role for appeals to experience in discerning doctrine, it was never a solitary role. The example in his work that is most likely to suggest the contrary is *The Doctrine of Original Sin*. We noted above that his Enlightenment rhetoric in this treatise verged on defending this doctrine on the basis of empirical observation alone, but we also saw that his later sermonic distillation made clear that he was actually appealing to experience to confirm central biblical teachings. As this might suggest, Wesley's use of the various resources for doctrinal reflection was ultimately *dialogical*. It was not a matter of simply using whichever resource seemed more helpful, or of playing one resource off against another, but of conferring among them until some consensus was found. His expectation of such consensus was based on the assumption that it is the same self-revealing God being encountered through Scripture, tradition, and experience—when each of these is rightly and rationally utilized.

Several desired contributions of experience to this dialogical process are evident in Wesley's various appeals. The most rudimentary contribution is help in clarifying the intended meaning of claims found in Scripture or tradition. An example would be his argument that Paul's claim "the love of money is the root of all evil" must mean only that it was the most prolific root of evil, not that it is the only root, because "sad experience daily shows" that there are a thousand other roots of evil in the world.[51]

A closely related contribution is testing possible interpretations of Scripture or tradition (including proposals for how to correlate apparently disparate claims within these sources). This is often what is taking place when Wesley appeals to experience to "confirm" a doctrine derived from Scripture.[52] Most of these appeals were on issues where his distinctive interpretation of Scripture was being challenged—such as, whether a sense of assurance is essential to justification, or whether believers continued to struggle with an inclination to sin.[53]

A third way that experience can contribute to the dialogue among the various resources is by suggesting and testing contextual applications of general principles found in Scripture or tradition. This contribution is implied in Wesley's response to a criticism that the band groups he instituted in Methodism were not biblical: "these are also prudential helps, grounded on reason and experience, in order to apply the general rules given in Scripture according to particular circumstances."[54]

Carrying this a step further, doctrinal issues can arise that are not addressed definitively in Scripture or earlier tradition, even in terms of principles. Wesley recognized that experience would have to play a fairly substantial role in deciding such issues. As a case in point, since he believed that Scripture was silent on the question of whether God works entire sanctification gradually or instantaneously, experience became his primary resource for settling it.[55]

One other dialogical contribution is evident in Wesley's various appeals to experience in doctrinal disputes. This contribution relates not to discerning whether a particular theological claim is acceptable, but whether it is central or essential to Christian faith. Between the poles of claims judged dangerously wrong and those considered essential to Christian faith, there have always been a range of theological suggestions that were deemed allowable "opinions" but judged unworthy of greater doctrinal endorsement. Wesley assumed that scriptural and traditional warrant played roles in discerning where specific theological proposals fit within this spectrum, but his distinctive emphasis was on experiential evaluation of how the proposal either helped nurture or undercut holiness of Christian life![56]

What kind of "experience" could provide such an evaluation? The first insight in answering this question is to note that Wesley's emphasis on experience in the sense of individual subjective consciousness stayed fairly confined to the role of empowering Christlike living. While this empowerment might flow in part from experience *confirming* Christian claims, Wesley specifically rejected the suggestion that he encouraged his followers to *derive* doctrine from such inner "feelings."[57] This comes through even in his sermons on the witness of the Spirit. While he presented the *event* of the witness as a matter of individual inward consciousness, his argument for affirming the *doctrine* of the witness of the Spirit started with his proposed scriptural warrant and then invoked the specifically corporate test of multiple public testimonies to verify his reading of Scripture.[58]

This focus on something public, corporate, and hopefully long-term was characteristic of Wesley's appeals to experience for purposes of doctrinal discernment. One form this took was his careful observation (as a "scientist" of spiritual realities) of the lives of his Methodist people and of the general populace. The best example is his prolonged consideration of the possibility for Christians to attain entire sanctification in this life. While Wesley believed that this possibility was affirmed in Scripture, he willingly acknowledged that if there were no living examples of attainment, his reading of Scripture would be suspect. This led him to inquire routinely into how many had claimed such attainment, whether their lives evidenced a depth of Christian love and holiness to match this claim, and whether this character persisted over time.[59]

The focus on a public, corporate, and long-term reality is even clearer when Wesley's appeals to experience involve the meaning of practical testing. These cases express his conviction that a central experiential test of disputed doctrinal issues is the long-term practical effects of each alternative in the life of the Christian community. To take just one example, he became increasingly vocal in rejecting the doctrine of unconditional election to salvation (and the interpretation of Scripture supporting it) because "repeated experience shows that it is not wholesome food—rather to [believers] it has the effect of deadly poison."[60]

Of course, simply making the *object* of his observation and practical testing corporate would not insulate Wesley from the potential distortions of his mediating preconceptions. He shows some awareness of this liability when he criticizes appeals to practical experience by his opponents for focusing too selectively in their consideration.[61] Though he never defended it in these exact terms, his emphasis on "conference" provided a means to help Wesley take this liability into account. Conference offered him access to other experiencing *subjects* who could test and enrich his preconceptions.

One way in which Wesley benefited from conference in doctrinal discernment was by consulting the seasoned wisdom of past saints.

As he acknowledged in the preface to his Sermons, he routinely turned to the writings of those departed ones who were "experienced in the things of God" when he struggled with how to understand something in Scripture.[62] In consulting such past figures Wesley was (largely unconsciously) challenging the Enlightenment's "prejudice against preunderstandings" that had blinded it to how it prejudicially favored the experience of contemporary socially privileged observers over all other human experience—past and present.[63]

His implicit challenge to Enlightenment assumptions went further as Wesley found his perspective enriched (often in unanticipated ways) by formal and informal conference with contemporaries from very different social settings than his own. As one case in point, his extended interaction with gifted women in his movement eventually discredited his inherited prescriptions against women preaching.[64] Likewise, his frequent immersion in the lives of the poor in his societies helped him to see economic matters in a new light. He remarked for example that he had "lately had more experience" concerning instances of wronging widows and orphans that caused him to reconsider his initial assumption that the majority of English merchants were honest.[65]

While these last examples should not be idealized, they support the insight that the experience which most benefited Wesley in doctrinal reflection was not the elite observational experience of the Enlightenment scholar, let alone the elite inner experience of certain caricatured forms of mysticism.[66] It was the pastoral wisdom that is nurtured by practical testing in the daily corporate life of the Christian community and is enriched by conferring broadly with the experience of others, past and present.

The Goad and Goal of Theological Reflection

There is one other major role of experience evident in Wesley's theological activity, and it also contrasts with confinement of theology to the elite of the academic community. This role is best seen in historical perspective. Early Christian doctrinal reflection emerged in intimate connection with daily Christian life. The central contributing figures were pastors seeking to help their flocks live more faithfully as Christians. As a result, the ongoing corporate life (i.e., the "experience") of the church served as the typical stimulus or goad, and the ultimate goal, of all their doctrinal reflection. Trained in an Anglican context with its emphasis on the precedent of the first four Christian centuries, Wesley imbibed this early model of theology. In keeping with the model, he tended to engage doctrinal issues only at the time, and to the extent, that they emerged within the ongoing life of the Methodist movement. And he insisted that the highest purpose of Christian doctrine was providing practical guidance for Christian life in the world. By contrast, Western academic theology more generally has progressively severed this connection of theology to the daily life of the Christian community. The end result is that academic theology today is largely written by scholars for scholars in response to scholarly questions, and is seldom read by pastors—let alone the broader community. This is not to say that professional theologians are happy with this situation! Many are seeking ways to reintegrate doctrinal reflection into the life of the church. In this search, Wesley's model of privileging the daily corporate life of the Christian community as the *goad* and *goal* of (as well as an important *guide* in) doctrinal reflection is receiving new appreciation.[67]

Experience as Dialogical Partner

We began by noting how present United Methodist debate over theological method tends to frame the issue in terms of a stark dichotomy between valuing *my* experience or accepting the tradition. By now it should be clear that this way of framing the issue reflects the impact of both the Enlightenment critique of tradition and the subsequent questioning of the Enlightenment's naive claim to absolute certainty. The perplexity created by this dual impact is how to avoid the besetting total relativism of post-Enlightenment culture without lapsing into uncritical traditionalism.

We have tried to show that we have a resource for addressing this perplexity in Wesley, with his dawning awareness of the limitations of Enlightenment certainty yet his refusal to embrace total relativism.[68] His way of dealing with this tension offers several potentially enriching counterpoints to tendencies in our present discussion, particularly in connection to the role of experience in Christian life and thought.[69]

To begin with, Wesley's recognition of the multi-faceted nature of "experience" calls into question the sharp contrast between experience and tradition that is so common in the current debate. This is particularly evident with the sense of experience as "seasoned wisdom." Such wisdom is a major component of tradition (including Scripture!). Thus, any adequate conception of the relation of experience and tradition must recognize overlaps alongside any contrasts.

This recognition calls into question the tendency of both sides in the current debate to view the role of experience in doctrinal discernment as that of an autonomous authority (which they either affirm or reject) weighing in against the authority of tradition or Scripture. Wesley's more dialogical model of the contribution of the various criteria to doctrinal discernment stands as a promising alternative for our consideration.

Just as the various criteria must be kept in dialogue with one another, Wesley stressed the necessity of conference within the community of faith as we seek to interpret and apply the criteria. His example puts a particular stress on including past voices in this conferring, which are often slighted today. At the same time he reached beyond academic professionals to bring others into the conference, including some of the excluded voices that are rightly the focus of concern today.[70] Such truly inclusive conference holds the best hope for helping contemporary United Methodists to recognize our own preconceptions and achieve some mutual accountability.

Finally, Wesley's overall practice of making the ongoing life of the Christian community the typical *goad*, a fruitful *guide*, and the ultimate *goal* of his doctrinal reflection stands in sharp contrast to the distance between our privatized experience and our professionally marginalized theology. Because United Methodists believe that God is present and speaking there, we have been at the forefront of those seeking to enrich our experience by including the experience of excluded contemporaries. If we were to add "Wesley's experience" to this mix, it could help in recovering a truly *enriching role of experience* in our lives and theology!

Conclusion

If you are one of those busy people who read the Introduction, then skimmed quickly over the intervening five chapters, or if you skipped immediately to these pages, the following are some of the essential points that you have missed in their detail. Perhaps these concluding pages will entice you to return to the "meatier" portions of our essays. At this juncture it is hopefully clear that the conjunction in our title, *Wesley **and** the Quadrilateral,* is a focus of contention in current United Methodist debates on theological method. Our efforts have been devoted to various dimensions of the issue concerning whether it is appropriate, or helpful, to speak of a Wesleyan Quadrilateral.

One dimension of this issue relates to identifying the Quadrilateral with Wesley, and it involves a specific set of questions: Was it a term that Wesley used? Are the four criteria of theological reflection named by this term evident in Wesley's own theological activity? And if so, was this something distinctive of Wesley's approach to theological reflection? We have conceded from the beginning that Wesley never used the term "quadrilateral"; however, chapters two through five have demonstrated the roles that consideration of Scripture, tradition (as least the early church and Anglican standards), reason (in its limited role as a tool of reflection), and experience (in its manifold senses) played in Wesley's theological activity. If the term "quadrilateral" is intended simply to affirm some self-conscious awareness of the role of all four of these elements in theological reflection, then it would seem appropriate to speak of Wesley as embracing the Quadrilateral.

In the opening chapter on the "middle way" we learned that The United Methodist Church did not invent the use of tradition and reason as ways through which the church came to interpret and understand Scripture. Although it began much earlier in other theological contexts, we outlined a process beginning in the mid-sixteenth century and continuing in almost soap opera-like fashion for nearly one hundred years. We discerned that this multi-partnered, conversational way of theologizing has a venerable history,with roots that are deeply entwined in the intrigue surrounding a succession of English monarchs. We looked at this story in more historical detail than was theologically necessary in order to make a specific point: theological issues have rarely been decided in the history of the church through abstract theologizing; they are rooted in the lives of people who are highly involved in the life of the church. This did not cease to be so when we left the stories of Henry VIII, Queen Mary, and Queen Elizabeth I, turning our attention more narrowly to Archbishops and theologians—Thomas Cranmer, John Jewel, Richard Hooker, and Thomas Cartwright. The English Church was struggling to develop what came to be its Anglican identity. This had to be delineated first in contrast with Roman Catholicism, the task of John Jewel, and then in comparison with the Puritans, a job essentially reserved for Richard Hooker, in debate with the Puritans, especially Thomas Cartwright. And all of these conversations were carried out in careful continuity with the theological precepts initially laid out by Thomas Cranmer.

The foundational principle from the very beginning of the discussion is that Scripture is *primary*. Thomas Cranmer began with this in his Preface to *The Great Bible*. John Jewel, in his *Apology* distinguishing the English Church from the Roman Church, made it clear that the English were not forsaking tradition, but they were putting Scripture first in a way that it seemed the Roman Church had forgotten. When Richard Hooker engaged the Puritans, both were in agreement about the primacy of Scripture, but they were in disagreement about what it means to put Scripture *first*. The Puritans believed that Scripture was authoritative comprehensively, including such issues as church governance, liturgical garb, etc. In his *Laws of Ecclesiastical Polity*, Hooker attempted to demonstrate that it was more reasonable to interpret the primacy of Scripture as the foundational authority for all *soteriological* issues. In other areas, especially where Scripture is silent about specific issues, the practices of tradition may be allowed. The Anglican theological heritage that Wesley inherited affirmed that Scripture was foundational and primary; that tradition, especially the earliest Christian centuries, was doctrinally trustworthy; that where Scripture did not specifically prohibit, tradition and reason could be used to formulate ecclesial law and practice; and finally, that sermons and liturgy were to be developed and practiced in such a manner as to be "experienced" by the congregants. We concluded that this way of theologizing was more than a "middle way" between the opposing sides of Roman Catholicism and Puritan Protestantism; it was a new and distinct way.[1] This Anglican precedent was also surely the source for Wesley's own theological sensitivity to the roles of tradition, reason, and experience alongside that of Scripture in theological reflection. As such, the basic fourfold commitment of the Quadrilateral was less *distinctive* of Wesley than *characteristic* of him as one nurtured in his Anglican context.

This recognition leads us to the second dimension of the issue concerning the appropriateness or helpfulness of speaking of a Wesleyan Quadrilateral. In this dimension the question shifts from whether there was a Quadrilateral in Wesley to whether any particular conception of the Quadrilateral is more true to Wesley (and more adequate for his contemporary heirs). That is, attention moves from simply affirming a role for Scripture, tradition, reason, and experience in theological reflection to considering the specific *nature* of each of these elements and their *relative contribution* to the overall theological task. These latter matters were the focus of chapters two through five.

Our concern in chapter two was to reclaim Wesley's nuanced conviction of the primacy of Scripture in all of Christian life, including theological decision-making. This task involved mapping Wesley's various uses of Scripture and surveying his self-conscious interpretive principles. There is an underlying premise in our chapter on Scripture, and it would read like this: If United Methodists generally speaking have interpreted *The Book of Discipline* to mean the Scriptures are our foundational and primary authority in theology, faith, and practice, we have not done a very good job of making this clear to our constituencies. When a Bishop writes in *The United Methodist Reporter* that tradition, reason, and experience "outvote" Scripture three-to-one on a sensitive social issue, and when that same paper, the primary source of news articles for Annual Conference newspapers, carries an article attempting to interpret the "Wesleyan Quadrilateral" in which the editor asserts that the Promise Keepers can get the Methodists on board and achieve their goal of "Biblical unity" if they will "use Scripture less," we have something afoot that would make real waves at a Conference chaired by a Lazarus-like John Wesley.

When John Wesley said that he was *homo unius libri*, he said this as an Anglican and not as a Puritan. Wesley sounded like a Puritan

Biblicist when he affirmed the authority of Scripture, but he did not theologize and develop ecclesial practices by looking in the Bible to see if he could find a textual warrant for every detail. For John Wesley the central purpose of Scripture was soteriological, and every doctrinal affirmation that is related to this saving truth is rooted in Scripture, even if it is not specifically formulated in Scripture. When attempting to exegete especially difficult passages, Wesley returned to a precept that he had learned from Susanna Wesley, rooted perhaps in Romans 12:6, and interpreted the difficult passages "according to the analogy of faith." While this Romans passage is usually translated and interpreted to mean "in proportion to one's faith," Wesley meant something more comprehensive than this. He intended that Scripture should be interpreted "according to the wholeness of Scripture," and this is fundamentally a salvific wholeness. The prophetic and apostolic intention of the Bible is that the people who come under its teaching will know the saving reality of God. On this terrain Scripture is authority without peer. On this point Wesley is at one both with his Anglican forbears and with the magisterial Reformers. In order to carry out this "rule" of Scripture, we described how Wesley used seven interpretive principles.

Having said all this, we recognize and affirm that Wesley did not theologize using Scripture "completely alone." The other components of the Quadrilateral have a place, but their place is *never* to subordinate or replace Scripture. In affirming that any particular passage must be read in light of the analogy of faith, Wesley was guarding against both simplistic proof-texting and idiosyncratic interpretation. This was particularly the case since confident decisions about what constituted the analogy of faith would be a communal matter, i.e., a matter of "conference." Of course, what conference actually provides is access to the wisdom of tradition, the benefit of others' experience, and reasoned interrogation. This recognition does not undermine the foundational authority of Scripture but highlights its mutual interdependence with the other aspects of the Quadrilateral. If we may risk a conjecture, we do not believe that Mr. Wesley would find it extraordinarily difficult to make his "interpretative way" amid the complexities and vagaries of modern biblical studies. In and through all of it, Wesley would continue to say that in the pages of The Book, God is speaking to us, and we must never stop reading and studying that Book.

When we turned to "tradition," it was important for us to point out that there is no such thing as a simple, straightforward definition of the word. By Wesley's time there were at least three possible definitions and uses for tradition, often referred to as "ancient authorities." (1) Anglicans, Puritans, and others all used quotations from ancient Christian authorities to refute the teachings of their opponents, but this definition of "ancient authorities" seems to have been reserved almost exclusively for canonical tradition. (2) The conservative Anglicans, often referred to as "Caroline divines," called on ancient authorities to defend their Church's theological teachings as well as their ecclesial practices. It seems to have been their intention to preserve a sense of *unbroken continuity* for the Anglican Church with the catholic (universal) church. (3) A third group of Anglicans appealed to ancient authorities in a more "programmatic" manner in order to give rationale and justification for the validity of certain programs for renewal in the life of the Church. It is in this third category that Wesley seems to fit best, although he was not reticent to use the other categories of definition.

In our contemporary setting, we tend to use tradition in an even more specific manner than any of the above, implying that the word denotes a definite cognitive and normative content. Wesley used the word to imply a definition similar to this on occasion, but it does not seem to have been his primary usage. Wesley's preference was to use tradition in reference to the earliest church, as being the purest when it was nearest its apostolic roots. It is here that he believed Christians had expressed the saving reality of God most clearly, and this could be discerned the best in their spiritual practices and disciplines. When he came to understand that it was virtually impossible to trace unbroken lines of *theological* purity from the earliest church, he increasingly nuanced the authority of the early Christian tradition more in the sense of their spiritual and moral purity than in their representation of a consensus of doctrine. This sense of antiquity's authority as lying in the purity of the church's *life* accords with Wesley's general concern in the revival period for illustrating the "way of salvation," and especially the life of holiness.

When we note that Wesley moved from emphasizing a consensus on doctrinal purity to an affirmation of moral and spiritual purity, this does not mean that he ceased to believe in the doctrinal purity of the earliest sources, only that he came to see that one could not actually trace a line of doctrinal purity from his day back to the earliest days of the church. In fact, Wesley's affirmation was that the doctrinal affirmations of the Anglican Church, the Articles of Religion, best reflected the purity of the apostolic faith—the same "scriptural primitive religion of love, which is now reviving throughout the three kingdoms," "the most scriptural national church in the world." So Wesley believed without reservation that Methodism was a "revival" of the apostolic faith expressed in the Bible, continued in the ancient church, and contained in the foundational theological documents of the Church of England. He believed that Methodism, being a faithful expression of the best in Anglicanism, was a fresh new medium through which God was speaking. The retrieval of our own "tradition" may be helpful to us in this regard, but we must be careful not to uncritically idealize the past as we seek a shared basis from tradition on which to go forward.

In chapter four we turned to "reason." If there is one significant thread that has held together our modern era, it is the seemingly unbounded confidence in "reason." Who wishes to deny the use of their reason, or who would want to be described as unreasonable? And John Wesley was prone to repeat often, "All reasonable people believe. . . ." These popular definitions and expressions are not unrelated to "reason" as a component of the Quadrilateral, but they are not really at the heart of the issue. Reason functions differently from any of the other components, more as a "tool" to work *with* information rather than as a source *from which* to draw information. This tool of reason may be applied to Scripture, tradition, and experience in order to understand them. As a matter of fact, we could not understand them without reason. So it is not surprising that Wesley appealed to the authority of reason more often than any other, with the exception of Scripture—and he quite often linked the two of them together. When Wesley was accused of religious "enthusiasm" or fanaticism, he wrote responses claiming to be a "reasonable enthusiast." His penchant for being reasonable and having a reason for everything is perhaps best summed up by his father in a letter to Susanna: "I think our Jack would not attend to the most pressing necessities of nature unless he could give a reason for it." During Wesley's university years his interest in reason led him to tutor his students at Lincoln College in "logic," and he admonished his Methodist pastors that logic is "necessary next, and in order to, the knowledge of the Scripture itself." In this unbridled confidence in the reasonableness of Christianity, Wesley was preeminently a child of the Enlightenment era.

In giving a formal definition to reason, it is important to note that Wesley rejected the classical notion that reason can find within itself eternal truths that transcend our ordinary experience. This concept had been expressed theologically in the teaching that God implanted truth in the human mind as "innate" ideas, and it is the task of reason to rationally discern these eternal, unchangeable concepts. Although Wesley rejected the Platonic notion of innate ideas, he affirmed reason's capacity as a tool for understanding. This capacity is exercised in three ways: by simple apprehension, by judgment, and by discourse. The step of apprehension is simply taking in or apprehending the information or data that is presented to the five senses. The stage of judgment processes the new data in comparison to old data, comparing, contrasting, and judging. In the final stage of discourse, the mind begins to think actively with the data, not only sorting and categorizing the old and new data, but possibly thinking of mediating ideas or conceiving imaginative alternatives.

By definition this means that Wesley was an empiricist, but he was actually an empiricist with a Platonic twist. Although he rejected the tenet of innate ideas that are divine, eternal truths available to rational discernment, Wesley affirmed that God *graciously* gives "spiritual senses" to believers, enabling them to see, hear, and taste the spiritual realm, to know and feel the presence of God. In a curious blend of "sensory information" and "eternal realities," Wesley developed a "transcendental empiricism." Through graciously endowed spiritual senses, the believer is able to discern, know, and experience the reality of God.

This brings us to the question whether Wesley really shared the unbounded confidence in reason that characterized the Enlightenment? The answer is, "No." Reason can only carry us so far; it has definite limits. Without the revelation of Scripture and without faith, reason cannot produce the things most essential to the Christian life. Also, it is subject to error and can never, this side of eternity, reach *full* knowledge of the spiritual realm. Those who would claim that their "spiritual senses" have given them a privileged perspective on the truth and activity of God would be reminded by Mr. Wesley, the "reasonable enthusiast," that God is not irrational and neither are God's ways with us.

We are now said to live in a "postmodern" world in which reason is no longer held in uncritically high esteem, and we cannot avoid asking whether the reasonable Mr. Wesley has anything to say to us in this "postrationalist" era. Perhaps the most important thing that he would say to us is what he said when confronted with pastoral situations that tested the limits of his reason. He cautioned his hearers to turn from "evil" or "idle" reasoning to a complete trust in God. He did not say, "Turn to the creeds." He did not even say, "Turn to Scripture." His admonition was, "Turn to God." In this turning you will hear again the voice that is foundational to your life. For Wesley it was reasonable to assert that you will experience God when you return to God.

In our final chapter examining "experience," we found the definition of experience illustrated in the previous paragraph to be one of the signal meanings attached to the word in early Methodism. There were, in fact, at least six distinct conceptions of experience: (1) conscious awareness of being affected by an encounter, event, or action; (2) sympathetic understanding derived from similar subjective experience; (3) practical skill developed through repeated performance; (4) practical/moral wisdom derived from life-long learning; (5) the act of putting to a practical test or trial as means of determining truth; and (6) verifiable observation of facts or events, as a source of knowledge. All these were used at one time or another in discernible ways in Wesley's writings, so it is not exactly simple to say that a Wesleyan use of the Quadrilateral must include experience.

When we add the mix of a typical use of "experience" in our contemporary setting, the issues are not simplified. It is commonplace for us to hear or say, "Well, that is your experience. Why does your experience give you the privilege of being so certain that you are right?" In this example experience is taken to result in a particular perspective, and all perspectives are taken as being relatively equal. This is not a new problem. It was confronted at least as early as the philosopher, Immanuel Kant, in his thesis: all human experience is *interpreted* experience, because it is *mediated* through our preexisting intellectual concepts. In his own day Kant offset the implied skepticism in his thesis by focusing on intepretive concepts that he believed to be universally shared and invariant, like space and time. Even before Einstein rendered these categories in their Newtonian formulations obsolete, sociologists and psychologists had already begun a process of demonstrating that all perspectives are conditioned. The net result of this for us is that in popular culture we have reduced experience to perspective. The obvious questions about (1) whether my perspective corresponds in any way to how things truly are, and

(2) what claim it has against other varying perspectives, are at the heart of the vigorous debates going on in late twentieth-century Western culture—to say nothing of the debates within The United Methodist Church. Does Wesley have anything to offer here? We believe that he does.

Perhaps the earliest example of a dawning awareness on Wesley's part of the mediated nature of human experience is in his sermonic distillation of the treatise on *The Doctrine of Original Sin.* The original treatise could serve as a showcase of Enlightenment optimism, especially when he concludes that the universality of sin should be obvious to "even the most careless, inaccurate observer." But in his sermonic distillation, Wesley renuances his perspective and concludes that those who have not been regenerated by God's grace typically do not discern the universality of sin. In other words, he concedes that empirical observation is not as immediately or publicly verifiable as his earlier treatise suggested.

To be sure, this concession does not rule out the continuing optimistic assumption that all who have received the benefits of regeneration discern God's truth and God's work in their lives immediately, thereby enabling them to render objective and categorical knowledge. If Wesley was holding on to such an assumption at this point (1759), ongoing reflection upon his journey was rapidly undercutting it. This can be illustrated by his changing evaluation of the role of Aldersgate within that journey. A variety of factors helped Wesley to recognize how certain instilled expectations had influenced his initial interpretation of what he experienced at Aldersgate, and the correlated negative assessment of his spiritual status before that event. As he progressively decided that several of these expectations were unwarranted or unwise, he was compelled to offer a revised interpretation of the role of Aldersgate in his spiritual pilgrimage. In this act of revising Wesley was conceding—at least implicitly—that not even the regenerate can avoid having their experience mediated through their preexisting expectations and conceptions.

The temptation to total skepticism that is implied when we recognize the "conditionedness" of our knowledge through experience is usually avoided for a very practical reason: it is not viable to be a total skeptic. What **is** common among us is to invoke the perspectival nature of mediated experience as a preemptive shield: "That is only *your* perspective. I am entitled to *my own!*" While Wesley did not hear this particular modern response in his day, he does potentially provide a way through the impasse—he continually exhorted the early Methodists about the importance of "Christian conference," specifically for nurturing lives of holiness and for deciding debated issues in theology. No one person's perspective was to be privileged over another's, and the collective perspective of all gave the advantage of a mutually arrived at conclusion.

For Wesley there was not only the collective wisdom of the present, there was also the collective wisdom of the past. To make this wisdom available he republished numerous spiritual biographies of saints through the ages as models to be imitated, and he gathered many of their written proverbs and manuals for spiritual formation in his fifty-volume *Christian Library*. He also cited them repeatedly. One insight we can gain from Wesley in this regard is that he assumed gathering and sharing this type of experience, a practice for which there was strong precedent in early Christianity, was a central task of theology! By contrast the historical course of Western academic theology has progressively separated materials devoted to sharing wisdom about spiritual guidance and formation from those devoted to a more formal consideration of doctrine—and denied the former truly theological status. From a Wesleyan perspective, this must be seen as one of the major weaknesses of contemporary theology, and Wesley would say to us that the people called Methodists should be at the center of attempts to reclaim a model of theology that is enriched by practical, spiritual wisdom.

When we come to the question whether experience can aid us in deciding theological debates, we have come to a real "sticky wicket." Actually, the question should probably not be whether experience can help demonstrate the truth of established Christian teachings (i.e., the Articles of Faith), but the logically prior issue of how it might help the church decide what to *keep teaching*. Wesley's pastoral role in the Methodist movement positioned him to confront the task of doctrinal discernment often—both in justifying to the larger church why Methodists should keep teaching their distinctive claims and in assessing the unconventional currents within his movement. In addition to the distinctive role for Scripture, tradition, and reason in this regard, Wesley also appealed to experience in this capacity. This appeal to experience in determining what Methodists should continue to teach and emphasize, however, was never for experience in a *solitary* role. It was always for the dialogical role of experience—in conversation with Scripture, tradition, and reason. When cases arose in which neither Scripture nor tradition seemed to provide comprehensive and compelling evidence (as in the distinctive early Methodist question whether God works entire sanctification gradually or instantaneously), experience became a compelling criterion for settling the issue.

One other dialogical contribution is evident in Wesley's various appeals to experience in doctrinal disputes. This relates not to discerning whether a particular theological claim is acceptable, but whether it is *central* or *essential* to Christian faith. Wesley assumed that our reason would help us discern through scriptural and traditional warrant what teaching fits best in the continuum from central and essential to *allowable*, but these warrants from Scripture and reason were not in and of themselves decisive. The final opinion rested on the experiential evaluation of how the theological teaching either helped nurture or undercut holiness of heart and life.

These kinds of emphases in Wesley's teachings on experience reflect that he had remained in close connection with the manner in which theology had been developed in the early centuries of the Christian Church—in intimate connection with daily Christian life. In keeping with this model, Wesley tended to engage doctrinal issues only at the time, and to the extent, that they emerged within the ongoing life of the Methodist movement. He insisted that the highest purpose of Christian doctrine was providing practical guidance for Christian life in the world. Wesley believed this to be God's design for experiential religion. In particular, Wesley's emphasis on conference takes on new significance in this light, as it forces us to test "our perspective" on experience against those of others. Advancing this a step further, the mediated nature of human experience would ultimately involve our perspective on the meaning of Scripture, tradition, and the "obvious" truths of reason as well. On these terms, the insistence on the interdependence of the Quadrilateral is actually a way of calling for an ongoing "conference" among Scripture, tradition, reason, and experience in theological reflection, set in the context of *our* ongoing conference with one another.

Such are some of our emphases regarding the individual elements of a truly *Wesleyan* Quadrilateral. It remains to develop our growing conviction about the vital interrelationship between the four components. We noted in the Introduction a tendency on both sides of the current debate to cast these elements into two opposing camps, Scripture and tradition versus reason and experience, typically assuming that one must ultimately opt for one pair or the other. Our explication of the ambiguities and overlaps of the various elements in chapters two through five was aimed at explaining why Wesley rejected such a forced option, and why this rejection remains cogent in our day. It is simply impossible to divide neatly between "theological" criteria and "philosophical" ones, or "epistemological" criteria and "canonical" ones, for instance, in order to play one set off against the other. What we believe is needed instead is a model of the relationship among these four criteria of theological reflection that is built on analogy with Wesley's insistence about the importance of *conference* for Christian life and teaching.

In contrast with both the antipolar contrast of Scripture and tradition with reason and experience in William Abraham and the "dialectical" model of relatively autonomous elements in John Cobb, we believe that a truly *Wesleyan* Quadrilateral will emphasize the *dialogical* relationship of Scripture, tradition, reason, and experience. By this we mean that authentic doctrinal reflection will not resort to simply using whichever criterion seems most amenable to one's preexisting assumptions, or to playing one criterion off against another. Instead, it will confer among the criteria concerning the issue in question until it finds consensus, or a way of honoring the integrity of all four. Obviously, this will not always be an easy or quick process. It will often mean living with ambiguity for as long as it takes our reasoned and prayerful reconsideration of Scripture, tradition, and experience to bear fruit in new possibilities.

One of the strengths that commends this dialogical model to us is that it helps us make sense of Wesley's simultaneous emphasis on (1) the primacy of Scripture, and (2) his insistence that we never have Scripture entirely alone. Wesley's defense of the primacy of Scripture was typically aimed at suggestions that (what he considered to be) the clear teaching of Scripture could be expected to capitulate to the claims of tradition, reason, or experience. Conversely, his disdain for extreme claims about "Scripture alone" was typically aimed at those who touted supposed teachings of Scripture over against broadly accepted affirmations of tradition, reason, and experience. In both cases, Wesley's obvious assumption was that appropriate "conference" among Scripture, tradition, reason, and experience would find a way to honor the integrity of each—often by refining the understanding of one or more!

Another reason for emphasizing the dialogical character of the Quadrilateral is that it can help reenforce the point that Scripture, tradition, reason, and experience are resources for ongoing doctrinal reflection. These four do not comprise the list of United Methodism's standard doctrinal affirmations; the latter are constititionally defined and protected in the *Discipline* as the Confession of Faith and the Articles of Religion. Our affirmation of the Quadrilateral is an endorsement of its balance as a "method" for bringing these doctrinal standards into conversation with the ongoing life of the church, not for replacing or setting them aside. Christians do not *believe in* Scripture, tradition, reason, or experience; we *believe in* the triune God, incarnate and revealed in Christ Jesus, present to us in the world through the Holy Spirit. The role of the former four elements of the Quadrilateral is to enable our encounter with that divine self-revelation and to continually refine our understandings of that encounter.

Wesley's (and our) commitment to the dialogue among Scripture, tradition, reason, and experience is of an ecumenical nature. At its best, theological reflection in all major Christian traditions approaches this dialogical ideal. To the question "How and why are we different?" perhaps our best response would be "We differ because we opt for different perspectives on the 'analogy of faith.'" Put in other terms, we bring different "orienting concerns" to the interpretation of Scripture, tradition, reason, and experience. In the Wesleyan tradition our orienting concern is soteriological. Thus, if we United Methodists wish our contemporary doctrinal reflection to stand in some continuity with Wesley (as the *Discipline* implies), we will not only seek to honor the dialogical integrity of the Quadrilateral, but we will also bear in mind Wesley's distinctive model, his orienting concern—namely, how God works salvifically in human life.

In our "Christian conference" we learned a lot from each other about what we agree to be a Wesleyan Quadrilateral. In the process we were reminded that we are least likely to entertain significantly new perspectives on our experience *or* our reading of Scripture and tradition when we talk only to ourselves. By contrast, in authentic dialogue with one another we were repeatedly challenged to, and supported in, important reconsiderations. A second point also became abundantly clear—United Methodists do have a Quadrilateral that is actively in use, although often not in ways that might be defined as Wesleyan. This leads us to commend, perhaps even *plead for*, an interpretation and use of the Quadrilateral within United Methodism that is more comprehensively Wesleyan, one in which Scripture is the rule and is authoritative in a way that should not be ascribed to the other components. Tradition, reason, and experience then form an interpretive or hermeneutical spiral in which the dialogical relationship among all the components continually enables the church to understand and apply Scripture more accurately and effectively. We understand the interrelationship among these four components to be "quadrilogical"—all are in conversation with each other. Tradition, reason, and experience help us to understand and explicate Scripture. At the same time, we remain continually open to Scripture's critique of our traditions, reasonings, and experiences—for we may not presume that we have ever heard *all* that Scripture, the normative source of God's self-disclosure, is saying to us.

In summary, the essential conclusion of our "conference" is this:

We believe that the Quadrilateral, when defined as "the rule of Scripture within the trilateral hermeneutic of tradition, reason, and experience," is a viable way of theologizing for United Methodism. We believe that this dialogical way of theologizing is in harmony with the teachings of John Wesley. And we believe that the theological application of this Neo-Wesleyan interpretation of the Quadrilateral is the most faithful way for The United Methodist Church to end the twentieth and begin the twenty-first century.

We invite other United Methodists to renew this conversation with us, with each other, and with our Wesleyan history and heritage.

Abbreviations

Wesley's works are cited, whenever possible, in the Bicentennial Edition of *The Works of John Wesley*. If the relevant volumes have not yet been published, then older editions are used. To facilitate the use of multiple editions, we have cited section numbers as provided by Wesley in some writings, especially the *Sermons*, and given dates for letters and *Journal* entries. References to the *Explanatory Notes Upon the New Testament* will be given only by book, chapter, and verse since most editions are unpaginated. The following abbreviations will be used to refer to these editions. When a work is cited in the notes without any other indication, Wesley's authorship is assumed.

Curnock   *The Journal of the Rev. John Wesley, A.M.*, edited by Nehemiah Curnock, 8 vols. (London: Epworth Press, 1909–1916).

Jackson   *The Works of the Rev. John Wesley, M.A.*, edited by Thomas Jackson, 3rd ed., 14 vols. (London: Wesleyan Methodist Book Room, 1872; often reprinted).

Journal   *The Journal of John Wesley*, in either Curnock or *Works*.

Notes   John Wesley, *Explanatory Notes Upon the New Testament* (London: William Bowyer, 1755; many later editions).

Sermons   John Wesley, *Sermons,* edited by Albert C. Outler; vols. 1–4 in *Works*.

Survey   *A Survey of the Wisdom of God in Creation*, edited by B. Mayor, 4 vols. (New York: N. Bangs and T. Mason, 1823).

Telford   *The Letters of the Rev. John Wesley, A.M.*, edited by John Telford, 8 vols. (London: Epworth Press, 1931).

Wesley   When this term is used without further qualification, it refers to John Wesley.

Works   *The Works of John Wesley*, begun as "The Oxford Edition of the Works of John Wesley" (Oxford: Clarendon Press, 1975–1983), continued as "The Bicentennial Edition of the Works of John Wesley" (Nashville: Abingdon Press, 1984—); 14 of 35 volumes published to date.

Notes

Notes to Introduction

1. See Ted Campbell, "The 'Wesleyan Quadrilateral': The Story of a Modern Methodist Myth," in Thomas A. Langford, ed., *Doctrine and Theology in The United Methodist Church* (Nashville: Kingswood Books, 1991), 154–61. More background for the following summary may be found in this essay.

2. See the first-hand reflections in Bob Parrott, ed., *Albert Outler: The Churchman*, (Anderson, IN: Bristol House, 1995), 92, 370ff., 460ff.

3. See the discussion of this revision in the essays collected in Langford, *Doctrine and Theology*.

4. John B. Cobb, Jr., *Grace and Responsibility: A Wesleyan Theology for Today* (Nashville: Abingdon Press, 1995), esp. 155–76. References are to 162, 173–75, and 9, respectively.

5. William J. Abraham, *Waking from Doctrinal Amnesia: The Healing of Doctrine in The United Methodist Church* (Nashville: Abingdon Press, 1995), esp. 56–65. References are to 63, 61, 45, and 104.

Notes to Chapter One

1. Linguistically it is probably more proper to translate the feminine form of *medius* as "middle of," thus rendering *via media* as "middle of the road" or "middle of the way."

2. Even in the recent work of so meticulous an historian as Richard Heitzenrater we read phrases like "Elizabeth, whose political savvy and religious inclinations (or lack thereof) led to the Elizabethan Settlement," and "Elizabeth's role in this process was not determined so much by strong personal religious sentiments, if indeed she had any, as by her political astuteness; she was . . . thoroughly *politique*." Cf. *Wesley and the People Called Methodists* (Nashville: Abingdon Press, 1995), 6, 8.

3. Perhaps the best and most concise historical essays on this entire era may be found in J. R. H. Moorman, *A History of the Church in England* (New York: Morehouse Barlow, 1973).

4. Cf. Preface to the Book of Common Prayer (1549 edition), "Concerning the Service of the Church."

5. I am indebted for the clarification of these needed innovations to Moorman's discussion of "Liturgical Innovations," 187ff.

6. See especially, E. J. Bicknell, *A Theological Introduction to the Thirty-nine Articles* (London: Longmans, Green and Co., 1944), 12–17.

7. For a full description of these documents and events, see Henry Gee and William J. Hardy, eds., *Documents Illustrative of English Church History* (London: Macmillan, 1921), 384–415.

8. For a discussion of this, see John Strype, *Ecclesiastical Memorials, Relating Chiefly to Religion. . .* , 3 vols. (London: Printed for John Wyatt, 1721), 3:232ff.

9. Gee and Hardy, *Documents*, 442–58; extracts in J. R. Tanner, ed.,, *Tudor Constitutional Documents, A.D. 1485–1603* (Cambridge: Cambridge University Press, 1930), 130–35.

10. Gee and Hardy, *Documents*, 458–67; Tanner, *Tudor Constitutional Documents*, 135–39.

11. Gee and Hardy, *Documents*, 417–42.

12. Cited by Henry R. McAdoo, *The Unity of Anglicanism: Catholic and Reformed* (Wilton, CT: Morehouse, 1983), 10.

13. Cf. J. P. Hodges, *The Nature of The Lion: Elizabeth I and Our Anglican Heritage* (London: Faith Press, 1962).

14. The key passages of the bull are reproduced in G. W. Prothero, ed., *Select Statutes and Other Constitutional Documents Illustrative of the Reigns of Elizabeth and James I*, 4th ed. (Oxford: Clarendon Press, 1913), 195–96; an English translation is given in Tanner, *Tudor Constitutional Documents*, 143–46.

15. Quotation from "An Admonition to Parliament" (1572), cited by W. H. Frere, *The English Church in the Reigns of Elizabeth and James I (1558–1625)* (London and New York: Macmillan, 1904), 179.

16. John Jewel, *An Apology of the Church of England*, ed. John Booty (Ithaca, NY: Cornell University Press for the Folger Shakespeare Library, 1963), 30.

17. The Great Bible (1539), Preface, 4; in *The Great Bible: A Facsimile of the 1539 Edition*, with introduction by Yoshio Teresawa (Tokyo: Elpis Co., Ltd., 1991), xxix.

18. Ibid., 5; *Facsimile Edition*, xxx.

19. Ibid., 6; *Facsimile Edition*, xxxi.

20. Cf. *The Sermons and Remains of Hugh Latimer*, ed. by G. E. Corrie for the Parker Society, 2 vols. (Cambridge: Cambridge University Press, 1844–45).

21. Latimer, *Sermons*, 1:61–62. "Of the Plough" was preached in London on 18 January 1548.

22. Ibid., 1:306.

23. Edmund Grindal, *The Remains of Edmund Grindal, Successively Bishop of London and Arshbishop of York and Canterbury*, ed. by William Nicholson for the Parker Society (Cambridge: Cambridge University Press, 1843), 382. The "Letter to the Queen" is dated 20 December 1576.

24. Jewel, *Apology*, 17.

25. Ibid., 120–21.

26. Horton Davies, *Worship and Theology in England*, Volume 1: *From Cranmer to Hooker, 1534-1603* (Princeton: Princeton University Press, 1970), 17.

27. Latimer, *Sermons*, 1:218.

28. Thomas Becon, *Prayers and Other Pieces of Thomas Becon*, ed. by John Ayre for the Parker Society (Cambridge: Cambridge University Press, 1844), 390.

29. Cited by John Whitgift, *The Defence of the Answer to the Admonition Against the Reply of T. C.* [drawn from Cartwright's *Admonition*, ¶14, §3], in *The Works of John Whitgift*, ed. by John Ayre for the Parker Society, 3 vols. (Cambridge: Cambridge University Press, 1851–53), 1:190.

30. Ames's *Medulla theologica*, published in Amsterdam in 1623, was the fruit of Ames's lectures to the sons of Leyden merchants. It was followed by twelve Latin printings; three printings of an English translation appeared between 1638 and 1643. The best modern English translation with historical introduction is by John D. Eusden, *The Marrow of Theology, William Ames, 1576–1633* (Boston: Pilgrim Press, 1968).

31. Richard Hooker, *Of the Laws of Ecclesiastical Polity*, I.xiv.1. Essentially all of Book I, Chapter xiv, revolves on the soteriological axis. The best available edition is *The Folger Library Edition of the Works of Richard Hooker*, Georges Edelin et al., eds., 5 vols. (Cambridge, MA: The Belknap Press of Harvard University Press, 1977).

32. Ibid., II.viii.5.

33. For a discussion of Hooker on "law," see Henry R. McAdoo, *The Spirit of Anglicanism: A Survey of Anglican Theological Methodology in the Seventeenth Century* (New York: Charles Scribner's Sons, 1965), 6ff.

34. Hooker, *Laws*, I.viii.4–11.

35. Ibid., Preface, VII.3.

36. Ibid., Preface, II.7–10.

37. Ibid., I.iii.5.

38. Ibid., I.iii.1.

39. Ibid., I.xiv.1.

40. Ibid., I.xvi.1. The Aristotelian and Thomistic philosophical assumptions that undergird Hooker's conceptual framework will be self-evident to those who are familiar with classical philosophy and medieval theology.

41. Ibid., V.viii.2.

Notes to Chapter Two

1. Quoted in Colin W. Williams, *John Wesley's Theology Today* (New York and Nashville: Abingdon Press, 1960), 5.

2. See the editorial analysis in "Promise Keepers, UMC Can Learn from One Another," *The United Methodist Reporter* (8 November 1996), 2.

3. John Wesley, "Thoughts Upon Methodism," §1, *Works* 9:527.

4. See the Constitution, Part I of *The Book of Discipline of The United Methodist Church, 1996*, Division 2, Section III, and its interpretation on pp. 26–27.

5. *The Book of Discipline, 1996*, ¶61.

6. See Albert C. Outler, "The Wesleyan Quadrilateral—In John Wesley," 75–88, and Ted Campbell, "The 'Wesleyan Quadrilateral': The Story of a Modern Methodist Myth," 154–61, both in Thomas A. Langford, ed., *Doctrine and Theology in The United Methodist Church* (Nashville: Kingswood Books, 1991). See also Scott Jones, *John Wesley's Conception and Use of Scripture* (Nashville: Kingswood Books, 1995), 62–64.

7. See, among others, John B. Cobb, Jr., *Grace and Responsibility: A Wesleyan Theology for Today* (Nashville: Abingdon Press, 1995), and William J. Abraham, *Waking from Doctrinal Amnesia: The Healing of Doctrine in The United Methodist Church* (Nashville: Abingdon Press, 1995).

8. Preface to the 1746 edition of *Sermons on Several Occasions*, *Works* 1:105.

9. "On God's Vineyard," §I.1, *Works* 3:504.

10. See Jones, 129, 224–25, for a discussion of this sample.

11. His sources (in order of frequency within this sample) are Milton, Charles Wesley, Virgil, Horace, Matthew Prior, Alexander Pope, Isaac Watts, Plato, Diogenes Laertius, George Herbert, Ovid, Quintillian, Thomas Otway, Cicero, Homer, Seneca, Hadrian, James Thomson, Samuel Wesley, Samuel Wesley, Jr., Suetonius, Lucretius, L. Annaeus Florus, and John Dryden.

12. "The Principles of a Methodist Farther Explained," §V.4, *Works* 9:219.

13. "On Faith (Hebrews 11:6)," §I.8, *Works* 3:496. A similar point is made in *Popery Calmly Considered,* Jackson 10:141.

14. This is the same sample referred to in note 10 above.

15. §II.30, *Works* 2:121. The identification of the Scripture references is the work of the editors of the Bicentennial Edition.

16. *Works* 11:71.

17. §19, *Works* 11:369.

18. The index to the four volumes of sermons lists twenty-six uses of Hebrews 11:1. Of these, eight are explicit definitions of "faith." Volume 11 of the Bicentennial edition of the *Works* includes the Appeals and related letters; of nine uses of Hebrews 11:1 in that volume, four are explicit definitions.

19. §II.1, *Works* 2:160.

20. *A Farther Appeal to Men of Reason and Religion*, Part I (1745), §I.4, *Works* 11:106–7. The quotations are from 2 Corinthians 5:19 and Galatians 2:20.

21. Ibid., §70, *Works* 11:75. Wesley is referring to Acts 18:7 and Acts 19:9.

22. John 3:3.

23. Cf. Romans 8:13.

24. 1 Thessalonians 5:22.

25. Titus 2:14.

26. Cf. Galatians 6:10.

27. Cf. Luke 1:6.

28. See John 4:23, 24.

29. Cf. Matthew 16:24.

30. §I.8, *Works* 2:160. Notes 22–29 are from the Bicentennial Edition.

31. 22 June 1763, Telford 4:216. The "little help from men" is a reference to his discussions with the Moravians in February, March, and April of 1738. Cf. *Journal* for 27 April 1738, *Works* 18:233–35.

32. "Christian Perfection," §2, *Works* 2:99–100. See a similar point in "The Law Established by Faith, II," §I.5, *Works* 2:37.

33. Letter to "John Smith" (28 September 1745), §5, *Works* 26:155.

34. *Works* 1:285–98.

35. §III.1, *Works* 1:288.

36. See "Christian Perfection," *Works* 2:99–124.

37. See Jones, 156.

38. *Notes*, Preface, §10.

39. *Notes*, Preface, §12.

40. See Jones, 19–21, 138–39 for a discussion of the places where this is true, notably in the *Notes* on Acts 15:7 and the preface to 1 Timothy.

41. Jackson 11:484.

42. Curnock 6:117.

43. §II.9, *Works* 3:527.

44. "Christian Perfection," §§1–3, *Works* 2:99–100.

45. §3, *Works* 2:100

46. *Notes*, Preface, §10.

47. *Notes*, Romans 12:6. The Scriptural references are to 1 Peter 4:11 and Jude 3.

48. §6, *Works* 4:89.

49. "The End of Christ's Coming," §III.5, *Works* 2:482.

50. For one of Wesley's most cogent statements of this way of salvation, see "The Scripture Way of Salvation," *Works* 2:153–69.

51. This translation is Wesley's, taken from the *Notes*. No other English versions of this passage use "analogy." For example, the AV uses "proportion" as do the NRSV and the NIV. However, the Greek word used is *analogion* and Protestant theologians have used "analogy of faith" as a technical term based on this passage. The NIV does have a footnote that offers the alternate reading "in agreement with the," which hints at this line of interpretation. For more detailed discussion, see Jones, 45–47.

52. "Free Grace," §20, *Works* 3:552.

53. §26, *Works* 3:556.

54. *Notes*, Matthew 25:3. The phrase "faith working by love" is a quotation from Galatians 5:6.

55. In suggesting this method, however, the Reformers were simply putting a new twist on a very old idea. As far back as Irenaeus Catholic commentators had referred to a "rule of faith" that should guide Christian teaching and preaching.

56. *Notes,* Romans 8:28.

57. *Works* 8:644.

58. See "An Address to the Clergy," §I.2, Jackson 10:482–84.

59. "Preface to *Hymns and Sacred Poems",* §5, Jackson 14:321. See also "Upon Our Lord's Sermon on the Mount, IV", §I.1, *Works* 1:533.

60. David Kelsey, *The Uses of Scripture in Recent Theology* (Philadelphia: Fortress Press, 1975) 106.

61. "On Laying the Foundation of the New Chapel," §II.1, *Works* 3:585.

Notes to Chapter Three

1. This chapter is based on a paper originally given in the Wesley Studies group of the 1987 Oxford Institute of Methodist Theological Studies. The paper was subsequently published in the *Anglican Theological Review* 74/1 (Winter 1992): 54–67 under the title "Christian Tradition, John Wesley, and Evangelicalism."

2. See Ted A. Campbell, *Christian Confessions: A Historical Introduction* (Louisville: Westminster/John Knox Press, 1996), 9–10.

3. See Ted A. Campbell, "Is It Just Nostalgia? The Renewal of Wesleyan Studies," *Christian Century* 107/13 (18 April 1990): 396–98.

4. Peter Gay, *The Enlightenment: An Interpretation,* Volume 1: *The Rise of Modern Paganism* (New York and London: W. W. Norton, 1966), 31–126.

5. John Wesley, "A Roman Catechism, with a Reply Thereunto," Jackson 10:86–128; cf. John Williams, *A Catechism Truly Representing the Doctrines and Practices of the Church of Rome, with an Answer Thereunto* (1686); cf. Ted Campbell, "John Wesley's Conceptions and Uses of Christian Antiquity" (Ph.D. dissertation, Southern Methodist University, 1984), 130–31.

6. A search of the CD-ROM version of the 14-volume Jackson edition of Wesley's *Works* shows twenty-seven occurrences of the word "tradition." Many of these refer to "heathen" traditions or "Scottish tradition." Quite a few refer to the merely human traditions ascribed to Roman Catholics in the "Roman Catechism, with a Reply Thereunto." Wesley's polemical opponent Conyers Middleton used the term to refer to the teachings of the ancient church, but Wesley's *A Letter to the Reverend Dr. Conyers Middleton* (Jackson 9:1–79) has the term only when quoting Middleton, not in Wesley's own comments. The so-called Wesleyan Quadrilateral understands "tradition" much in the way in which it was discussed in a World Council of Churches Faith and Order

Commission paper on "Scripture, Tradition, and Traditions" presented at Montreal in 1963. That paper recognized "Tradition" (with an upper-case "T") as "God's revelation and self-giving in Christ, present in the life of the Church," and "traditions" (here with the lower-case "t") as "the expressions and manifestations in diverse historical forms of the one truth and reality which is in Christ" (World Council of Churches, Faith and Order Commission, "Scripture, Tradition, and Traditions," pars. 46–47; in Hans-Georg Link, ed., *Apostolic Faith Today: A Handbook for Study* [Faith and Order Paper no. 124; Geneva: World Council of Churches, 1985], 82). Not surprisingly, Albert C. Outler was present at the Montreal Faith and Order Conference, and so the understanding of "tradition" as a part of the Wesleyan Quadrilateral derives from Outler's ecumenical contacts. This use of "tradition" must be borne in mind: a more exclusive definition would claim "tradition" to be those elements of the Christian past which not only bear a continuity with the Christian past, but which do so in a more or less unbroken succession. As I shall suggest later, Wesley often pits "tradition" (in the former sense) against "tradition" in this latter and more restricted sense.

7. "A Fruitful Exhortation to the Reading of the Holy Scripture," Part I; *Certain Sermons or Homilies Appointed to be Read in Churches in the Time of Queen Elizabeth of Famous Memory* (London: SPCK, 1890), 2.

8. Scott J. Jones, *Wesley's Conception and Use of Scripture* (Nashville: Kingswood Books, 1995), 81–94, 169–76, 222–23.

9. Albert C. Outler, "A New Future for Wesley Studies: An Agenda for 'Phase III,'" in M. Douglas Meeks, ed., *The Future of the Methodist Theological Traditions* (Nashville: Abingdon Press, 1985), 38–40.

10. Cited in Stanley Lawrence Greenslade, *The English Reformers and the Fathers of the Church* (Oxford: Clarendon Press, 1960), 8–9.

11. Richard Hooker, *Of the Laws of Ecclesiastical Polity*, V.6–9, in *The Folger Library Edition of the Works of Richard Hooker*, Georges Edelin, et al., eds., 5 vols. (Cambridge, MA: The Belknap Press of Harvard University Press, 1977), 2:32–46; cf. H. R. McAdoo, *The Spirit of Anglicanism: A Survey of Anglican Theological Methodology in the Seventeenth Century* (New York: Charles Scribner's Sons, 1965), 319–20; John K. Luoma, "Who Owns the Fathers? Hooker and Cartwright on the Authority of the Primitive Church," *Sixteenth Century Journal* 8 (1977): 53–58.

12. Lancelot Andrewes, *Opuscula quaedam posthumata*, The Library of Anglo-Catholic Theology (Oxford: John Henry Parker, 1852), 91; cf. McAdoo, *Spirit of Anglicanism*, 317–20.

13. See McAdoo, *Spirit of Anglicanism*, passim; Gerald R. Cragg, *Freedom and Authority: A Study of English Thought in the Early Seventeenth Century* (Philadelphia: The Westminster Press, 1975), 118–24.

14. Luoma, 48–53.

15. John [i.e., Jean] Daillé, *A Treatise concerning the Right Use of the Fathers* (London: John Martin, 1651; trans. Thomas Smith); see the "De-

signe of the whole Work," v–viii. This edition has a list of approbations from English divines representing the Tew Circle (ix–x); cf. McAdoo, 316.

16. William Cave, *Primitive Christianity: or, the Religion of the Ancient Christians in the First Ages of the Gospel* (London: Thomas Tegg, 1840), iii.

17. William Beveridge, ΣΥΝΟΔΙΚΟΝ, *sive Pandectae Canonum Ss. Apostolorum et Conciliorum Ecclesia graeca receptorum*, 2 vols. (Oxford: William Wells and Robert Scott, 1672); Beveridge, *Codex Canonum Ecclesiae primitivae vindicatus ac illustratus*, 2 vols. (Oxford: John Henry Parker, 1847); Nathaniel Marshall, *The Penitential Discipline of the Primitive Church* (Oxford: John Henry Parker, 1844).

18. George Bull, *Defensio Fidei Nicaenae: A Defense of the Nicene Creed, out of the Extant Writings of the Catholick Doctors, who Flourished during the First Three Centuries of the Christian Church*, 2 vols. (Oxford: John Henry Parker, 1851); cf. Bull, *The Judgment of the Catholic Church on the Necessity of Believing that our Lord Jesus Christ is Very God* (Oxford: John Henry Parker, 1855); John Pearson, *Vindiciae Epistolarum S. Ignatii*, 2 vols. (Oxford: John Henry Parker, 1852).

19. See the works by Cave, Beveridge, and Marshall cited above; on the Latitudinarians, see Edward Stillingfleet, *The Irenicum: or, Pacificator* (Philadelphia: M. Sorin, 1842) and Peter King, *An Enquiry into the Constitution, Discipline, Unity, and Worship of the Primitive Church* (New York: P. P. Sandford, 1841).

20. "On Laying the Foundation of the New Chapel, near the City Road, London," §II:3, *Sermons* 3:586.

21. "The Mystery of Iniquity" (1783), ¶¶23–28, *Sermons* 2:460–64; "Of Former Times" (1787), ¶¶15–17, *Sermons* 3:449–51.

22. "Salvation by Faith," §III:9, *Sermons* 1:129.

23. *A Farther Appeal to Men of Reason and Religion*, Part III, §III:12, *Works* 11:298.

24. "On Laying the Foundation. . . ," §II:1, *Sermons* 3:585.

25. Ibid., §II:2–4, *Sermons* 3:585–86.

26. "Farther Thoughts on Separation from the Church," ¶¶1–2, Jackson 13:272–74.

27. Samuel Wesley passed on to John two works suggesting a course of theological studies, in which the Caroline theologians figured prominently: *The Young Student's Library*, attributed to Samuel as president of the Athenian Society (London: John Dutton, 1692); and *Advice to a Young Clergyman, in a Letter to Him* (London: C. Rivington, 1735).

28. Cf. Thomas Lathbury, *A History of the Non-Jurors* (London: William Pickering, 1845), 309–61; Wesley had met a member of the Manchester group, John Clayton, in Oxford, and in the summer of 1733 traveled with Clayton to Manchester, where Wesley met Thomas Deacon. Deacon included a fragment of an essay by Wesley on the "stationary" fasts (the Wednesday and Friday fasts) in Deacon's *Compleat Collection of Devotions* (London: printed for the author, 1734), 72–74.

29. Manuscript fragment, apparently extending Wesley's *Journal* account for 24 January 1738, Curnock 1:419. This manuscript fragment is transcribed in Campbell, 321–23 (Appendix 2).

30. On Wesley's editions of these works, see Ted A. Campbell, *John Wesley and Christian Antiquity: Religious Vision and Cultural Change* (Nashville: Kingswood Books, 1991), 92–145.

31. "On Attending the Church Service," ¶14, *Sermons* 3:469–70; the Constantinian fall is also described in *A Letter to the Reverend Dr. Conyers Middleton*, ¶¶3–4, Jackson 10:1–2.

32. "On Laying the Foundation. . . ," §II:3, *Sermons* 3:586.

33. Cited by Wesley in the manuscript apparently extending the *Journal* account for 24 January 1738 (Curnock 1:419).

34. This manuscript fragment is transcribed in Campbell, *John Wesley and Christian Antiquity*, 321–23 (Appendix 2).

35. *Journal* for 13 September 1737, Curnock 1:274–75, and 20 September 1737, Curnock 1:276–78.

36. *Letter to . . . Middleton*, §VI.III.12, Jackson 10:79.

37. See the descriptions of these works in Campbell, *John Wesley and Christian Antiquity*, 108–9, 124–29.

38. This is reflected in the excerpt from August Gottlieb Spangenberg's diary cited in Martin Schmidt, *John Wesley: A Theological Biography*, trans. Norman Goldhawk and Denis Inman, 2 vols. in 3 (Nashville: Abingdon Press, 1963–73), 1:138 n. 6.

39. Frank Baker, *John Wesley and the Church of England* (Nashville: Abingdon Press, 1970), 41.

40. An example of this species of Wesleyana would be R. Denny Urlin's *Churchman's Life of Wesley*, rev. Ed. (London: SPCK, 1880).

41. *Journal* for 12 November 1738, Curnock 2:101.

42. See Albert C. Outler, *John Wesley*, A Library of Protestant Thought (New York: Oxford University Press, 1964), 121–33.

43. "On Laying the Foundation. . . ," §II:4, *Sermons* 3:586.

44. Letter "To our Brethren in America," ¶4, Telford 7:239. To this one may compare Wesley's general definition of the Church of England given in a manuscript cited by Frank Baker, *John Wesley and the Church of England*, 327: "that body of people, nominally united, which profess to uphold the doctrine contained in the Articles and *Homilies*, and to use Baptism, the Lord's Supper and Public Prayer, according to the Common Prayer Book."

45. "On Laying the Foundation. . . ," §II:4, *Sermons* 3:208 and n. 64.

46. "Farther Thoughts on Separation from the Church," ¶¶1–2 (Jackson 13:272–74).

47. "On Working Out Our Own Salvation," §III:7 *Sermons* 3:208 and n. 64.

48. A dialogue between John Wesley and Bishop Joseph Butler, reported by Henry Moore and given in Curnock 2:257; cf. Frank Baker,

"John Wesley and Bishop Joseph Butler: A Fragment of John Wesley's Manuscript Journal, 16th to 14th August 1793," *Proceedings of the Wesley Historical Society* 42 (May 1980): 97.

49. Letter "To a Member of the Society" (16 September 1774), Telford 6:113; letter to Dr. Erskine (24 April 1765), Telford 4:296; *Journal* for 14 January 1756, Curnock 4:145–46.

50. *The Sunday Service of the Methodists in North America* (London, 1784). In the prefatory letter to this work, Wesley asserted, "I BELIEVE there is no LITURGY in the World, either in ancient or modern language, which breathes more of a solid, scriptural, rational Piety, than the COMMON PRAYER of the CHURCH of ENGLAND" (p. A1).

51. "The General Spread of the Gospel," ¶¶1–15, *Sermons* 2:485–92.

52. "A Plain Account of the People Called Methodists," §I:10, §VI:5, and §III:1 (Jackson 8:250–51, 258–59, 255–56).

53. See, for example, the patristic material cited against Bishop Smalbroke in *A Farther Appeal to Men of Reason and Religion*, Part I, §V:15–23, *Works* 11:154–66.

54. An example would be the poem entitled "Primitive Christianity," which concludes *An Earnest Appeal to Men of Reason and Religion* (1743) and describes the ancient Christians' simplicity, constancy in prayer, fellowship, unity, and love for each other; see *Works* 11:90–94.

55. The Latin sermon translated by Adam Clarke entitled "True Christianity Defended" cites Archbishop John Tillotson and Bishop George Bull as teaching moralism in this sense: §I:5–6, *Sermons* 4:395–96, 410–11.

56. On the extracts from the Anglican Homilies, see Outler, *John Wesley*, 121–33; *A Farther Appeal to Men of Reason and Religion*, Part I, §II–V, *Works* 11:108–176.

Notes to Chapter Four

1. The best full-length study of Wesley's understanding and use of reason is Rex D. Matthews, "'Religion and Reason Joined': A Study in the Theology of John Wesley" (Th.D. diss., Harvard University, 1986). See also Randy L. Maddox, *Responsible Grace: John Wesley's Practical Theology* (Nashville: Kingswood Books, 1994), 26–47; Donald A. D. Thorsen, *The Wesleyan Quadrilateral: Scripture, Tradition, Reason and Experience as a Model of Evangelical Theology* (Grand Rapids, MI: Zondervan, 1990), 169–200; Lawrence W. Wood, "Wesley's Epistemology," *Wesleyan Theological Journal* 10 (1975): 48–59; Richard E. Brantley, *Locke, Wesley, and the Method of English Romanticism* (Gainesville, FL: University of Florida Press, 1984); and Scott J. Jones, *John Wesley's Conception and Use of Scripture* (Nashville: Kingswood Books, 1995), 65–80.

2. Letter to Dr. Thomas Rutherforth (28 March 1768), §III.4, *Works* 9:382.

3. "A Dialogue between An Antinomian and His Friend" (1745), Jackson 10:267.

4. *Journal* for 28 November 1750, *Works* 20:371.

5. *An Earnest Appeal to Men of Reason and Religion* (1743), §27, *Works* 11:55.

6. Letter to Joseph Benson (5 October 1770), Telford 5:203.

7. Thorsen, 127 and 276 n.2.

8. "The Nature of Enthusiasm," §26, *Works* 2:55–56; "Causes of the Inefficacy of Christianity," §12, *Works* 4:93; "Seek First the Kingdom," §6, *Works* 4:219; *A Farther Appeal to Men of Reason and Religion*, Part III, §§III.28–29, *Works* 11:310–11; *A Farther Appeal*, Part III, §III.5, *Works* 11:293; "The Principles of a Methodist Farther Explained," §§V:7–8, Jackson 8:467; and *A Letter to the Right Reverend the Lord Bishop of Gloucester* (1763), §II.18, *Works* 11:516–17. Wesley wrote, for example, that Methodists "prove the doctrines we preach by Scripture and reason; and, if, need be, by antiquity." *A Farther Appeal*, Part III, §III.28, *Works* 11:310. He often repeated this phrase to note the three authorities of Scripture, reason, and antiquity.

9. "Some Remarks on Mr. Hill's 'Review of All the Doctrines Taught by John Wesley'" (9 September 1772), Jackson 10:413.

10. *A Farther Appeal*, Part III, §III.29, *Works* 11:311.

11. Letter to Freeborn Garrettson (24 January 1789), Telford 8:112. Wesley claimed, indeed, that not only he, but Methodists generally, "have but one point in view—to be altogether Christians, scriptural, rational Christians." Letter to Mary Bishop (5 November 1769), Telford 5:154. Wesley also refers to "the plain, scriptural, rational way" in "The Nature of Enthusiasm," §26, *Works* 2:55–56.

12. See, for example, his letter to Dr. Thomas Rutherforth (28 March 1768), §III.4, *Works* 9:382. See also George White, "A Sermon Against the Methodists"; "A Letter from Mrs. Elizabeth Hutton," in Richard Heitzenrater, *The Elusive Mr. Wesley: John Wesley as Seen by Contemporaries and Biographers*, 2 vols. (Nashville: Abingdon Press, 1984), 2:65–68 and 75–77; and W. Stephen Gunter, *The Limits of 'Love Divine': John Wesley's Response to Antinomianism and Enthusiasm* (Nashville: Kingswood Books, 1989), chaps. 1–3.

13. The second syllable "thus" comes from *theos*, "god," and the word "theology," the study of God, shares the same root; see "enthusiasm" in *The Concise Oxford English Dictionary* (Oxford: Oxford University Press, 1976), 345. Wesley questioned this etymology. After examining and criticizing several possible origins, Wesley wrote, "Perhaps it is a fictitious word, invented from the noise which some of those made who were so affected." "The Nature of Enthusiasm," §6, *Works* 2:48.

14. "Enthusiast," Samuel Johnson, *A Dictionary of the English Language*, 6th ed., 2 vols. (London: J. F. and C. Rivington, 1785), quoted in Matthews, "Appendix," 380.

15. "The Nature of Enthusiasm," §12, *Works* 2:50.

16. Ibid.

17. "The Case of Reason Impartially Considered," §1, *Works* 2:587.

18. "The Nature of Enthusiasm," §11, *Works* 2:49.

19. Letter to Dr. Thomas Rutherforth (28 March 1768), §III.4, *Works* 9:382.

20. "The Case of Reason Impartially Considered," §1, *Works* 2:587.

21. Ibid. Not all the critics of reason sprang from enthusiast roots. Wesley was also suspicious of continental reformers who questioned reason. After reading Martin Luther's "Commentary on the Epistle to the Galatians," Wesley castigated himself for ever having recommended Luther's Commentary. He wrote, "I was utterly ashamed." Wesley gave two examples to show that Luther was not only "shallow . . . muddy and confused" but also "dangerously wrong." Wesley wrote, "How does he (almost in the words of Tauler) decry reason, right or wrong, as an irreconcilable enemy to the gospel of Christ! Whereas what is reason (the faculty so called) but the power of apprehending, judging, and discoursing? Which power is no more to be condemned in the gross than seeing, hearing, or feeling." See *Journal* for 15 June 1741, Jackson 1:315.

22. Gerald R. Cragg, *Reason and Authority in the Eighteenth Century* (Cambridge: Cambridge University Press, 1964), 156; quoted in Matthews, 6.

23. According to Richard Heitzenrater the first appearance of this quotation was in Adam Clarke's *Memoirs of the Wesley Family*; see Richard P. Heitzenrater, *The Elusive Mr. Wesley*, 2 vols. (Nashville: Abingdon Press, 1984), 2:177.

24. The original known source for this quotation is John Wesley himself; see his letter to Joseph Benson (5 October 1770), Telford 5:203.

25. *Journal* for 1 August 1742, *Works* 19:288, quoting a letter from Susanna Wesley (24 July 1732).

26. To illustrate the various kinds of arguments in his logic text, Wesley suggested that the reader examine several of his sermons that conform to formal patterns of logical argument. See *A Compendium of Logic*, Jackson 14:189. He refered to the sermons "The Means of Grace," *Works* 1:381, and "The Nature of Enthusiasm," *Works* 2:46–60.

27. "An Address to the Clergy," §I.2, Jackson 10:483.

28. Ibid., §I.1, Jackson 10:481.

29. Wesley chastised one of his preachers whose sermons lacked depth, and "variety," and "compass of thought." The cause, claimed Wesley, was a "want of reading." The only remedy for superficial preaching was to give a part of each day to reading and prayer. Letter to John Tremblath (17 August 1760), Telford 4:102.

30. "The Case of Reason Impartially Considered," §6, *Works* 2:589.

31. Ibid., §3, *Works* 2:588.

32. Ibid., §3 and §5, *Works* 2:588.

33. Ibid., §II.10, *Works* 2:599.

34. Ibid., §II.10, *Works* 2:600.

35. Ibid., §I.1, *Works* 2:589.

36. Letter to Samuel Wesley (22 May 1727), *Works* 25:222. Matthews (126–28) lists dozens of examples of Wesley's common use of reason as argument or motive.

37. "The Case of Reason Impartially Considered," §I.1, *Works* 2:589–90. See also "The Imperfection of Human Knowledge," §I.4, *Works* 2:571.

38. This argument is best seen in the work of Matthews, Maddox, Brantley, and Wood. The other side of the argument, Wesley's Platonism, is found in Outler's notes in *Sermons* 1:146 n. 54, 1:276 n. 46, 1:433 n. 7, 1:711 n. 122, 2:192 n. 29, and 2:571 n. 7; John C. English, "The Cambridge Platonists in John Wesley's Christian Library," *Proceedings* 37 (1970): 101–4; Roderick T. Leupp, "'The Art of God': Light and Darkness in the Thought of John Wesley" (Ph.D. diss., Drew University, 1985), 197–98, 224–29; and Mitsuo Shimizu, "Epistemology in the Thought of John Wesley" (Ph.D. diss., Drew University, 1980), 29 n. 1, 111–92, 219–24. For a good discussion of these two conflicting interpretations of Wesley, see Matthews, chapter four and Thorsen, chapter six.

39. "The Case of Reason Impartially Considered," §I.1, *Works* 2:590.

40. "The Imperfection of Human Knowledge," §I.4, *Works* 2:571.

41. "The Case of Reason Impartially Considered," §I.2, *Works* 2:590. See also *A Compendium of Logic*, Jackson 14:161.

42. "On the Discoveries of Faith," §1, *Works* 4:29. See also "Walking by Sight and Walking by Faith," §7, *Works* 4:51.

43. "The Case of Reason Impartially Considered," §I.2, *Works* 2:590. See also *A Compendium of Logic*, Jackson 14:161.

44. Ibid.

45. Ibid. See also "Remarks on Mr. Locke's Essay on Human Understanding," Jackson 13:455–64.

46. Ibid.

47. Wesley refers to these three operations or functions of reason as understanding in many places throughout his work. See, for example, *An Earnest Appeal*, §§31–32, *Works* 11:56–57. *Journal* for 15 June 1741, *Works* 19:201; "The General Deliverance," §I.5, *Works* 2:441; "A Word to a Drunkard," Jackson 11:169; and "Remarks Upon Mr. Locke's 'Essay on Human Understanding,'" Jackson 13:460–63. For further references, see Matthews, 140–42.

48. *A Compendium of Logic*, Jackson 14:161–89. The quotations above are straight from Wesley's translation of Aldrich. Wesley was also influenced by empiricism as it was articulated in the work of John Locke and Peter Browne.

49. For a complete discussion of this point, see Matthews, 247–312. Matthews counters earlier claims about Wesley's Platonist leanings and lays out a convincing argument that Wesley was finally an empiricist.

50. Through the spiritual senses, awakened by the Holy Spirit, humans can directly experience or sense the spiritual realm. This capacity will be explained more fully below.

51. "Walking by Sight and Walking by Faith," §7, *Works* 4:51. See also *An Earnest Appeal*, §32, *Works* 11:56; and "On the Discoveries of Faith," §1, *Works* 4:29.

52. See note 38 above.

53. "On Living Without God," §5, *Works* 4:169–76.

54. Ibid., §5, *Works* 4:170.

55. Ibid., §§9–11, *Works* 4:172–73.

56. "On Faith," §2, *Works* 4:189.

57. Ibid., §7, *Works* 4:192–93.

58. Of course, any claims about knowledge derived from the spiritual senses must be tested by Scripture and the other authorities. Wesley was always cautious about exaggerated claims for personal inspiration.

59. George C. Cell, *The Rediscovery of John Wesley* (New York: Henry Holt, 1935), 84–86, 168–94. See Matthews, 308–9, and Thorsen, 183–84 and 292 n. 65.

60. For a discussion of this point, see Jones, 66–67 and Maddox, *Responsible Grace*, 41.

61. See, for example, Wesley's letter to Robert Carr Blackenbury (9 March 1782), Jackson 13:3.

62. For the moment, we will set aside the question of whether or not *we* agree with Wesley about these "obvious" conclusions of all rational people. Certainly, many in our culture would disagree with him.

63. Wesley explores this question directly in "The Case of Reason Impartially Considered," §§I.3–II.10, *Works* 2:590–99.

64. "The Case of Reason Impartially Considered," §I.3, *Works* 2:590.

65. Ibid. See also "The Imperfection of Human Knowledge," §3, *Works* 2:569.

66. Ibid., §I.3, *Works* 2:590–91.

67. Ibid., §I.5, *Works* 2:591.

68. Ibid., §I.6, *Works* 2:591.

69. Ibid., §I.6, *Works* 2:591–92.

70. *A Farther Appeal*, Part II, §III.21, *Works* 11:268; "Upon our Lord's Sermon on the Mount, VI," §III.7, *Works* 1:580–81; "Walking by Sight and Walking by Faith," §8, *Works* 4:51–52; "On Working Out Our Own Salvation," §I.1, *Works* 3:199; and *Survey* 1:312–13 and 378.

71. "On Faith," §I.4, *Works* 3:494; *Survey* 1:312–13; "The Wisdom of God's Counsels," §§1–6, *Works* 3:552–54; *The Doctrine of Original Sin*, Section III, Jackson 9:322; "The Imperfection of Human Knowledge," §I.4, *Works* 2:571; and "Original Sin," §II.3, *Works* 2:177.

72. *Survey* 1:378.

73. *Survey* 1:312–13.

74. "On Faith," §I.4, *Works* 3:494; "Walking by Sight and Walking by

Faith," §7, *Works* 4:51; and "The Reward of Righteousness," §1, *Works* 3:400.

75. "The Case of Reason Impartially Considered," §II.2, *Works* 2:578. See also "On Divine Providence," §§1–4, *Works* 2:535–36.

76. Wesley often wrote about the human capacity to know the general attributes of God. See, for example, "Original Sin," §II.3, *Works* 2:177; "The Imperfection of Human Knowledge," §§I.1–3, *Works* 2:569–70; "On Faith," §I.4, *Works* 3:494; *Survey* 1:312; "The Wisdom of God's Counsels," §§1–6, *Works* 3:552–53; "Walking by Sight and Walking by Faith," §7, *Works* 4:51; "Salvation by Faith," §I.1, *Works* 1:119; and *A Farther Appeal*, Part II, §III.21, *Works* 11:268.

77. "On Working Out Our Own Salvation," §1, *Works* 2:199.

78. "Original Sin," §II.3, *Works* 2:177.

79. "The Case of Reason Impartially Considered," §I.13, *Works* 2:577.

80. Ibid. See also "The Imperfection of Human Knowledge," *Works* 2:568–85.

81. *An Earnest Appeal*, §14, *Works* 11:49. See also "On Conscience," *Works* 3:480–90; "Upon Our Lord's The Sermon on the Mount, V," §I.2, *Works* 1:551–52; *Survey* 2:449–50; "Salvation by Faith," §I.1, *Works* 1:119; "On Working Out Our Own Salvation," §1, *Works* 2:199; "The Original, Nature, Properties and Use of the Law," §§I.3–6, *Works* 2:7–8; "The Witness of Our Own Spirit," *Works* 1:300–13; and "Walking by Sight and Walking by Faith," §7, *Works* 4:51.

82. "The Original, Nature, Properties and Use of the Law," §I.3, *Works* 2:7.

83. Ibid., §I.4, *Works* 2:7.

84. "On Conscience," §§I.5 and 9, *Works* 3:482 and 484.

85. Wesley preferred to use the word "conscience" because it is more commonly used by Christians. For a discussion of his differences with Francis Hutchinson's model of the moral sense, see "On Conscience," §§I.5 and 9, *Works* 3:482 and 484.

86. "The Heavenly Treasure in Earthen Vessels," §I.1, *Works* 4:163.

87. Letter to Joseph Benson (17 September 1788), Telford 8:89.

88. "The Case of Reason Impartially Considered," §II.1, *Works* 2:593.

89. Ibid., §II.8, *Works* 2:598.

90. "The Imperfection of Human Knowledge," §2, *Works* 2:568–69.

91. "The Heavenly Treasure in Earthen Vessels," §II.1, *Works* 4:165.

92. See, for example, *A Letter to the Right Reverend the Lord Bishop of Gloucester* (1763), §I.6, *Works* 11:502; *Journal* for 31 December 1739, *Works* 19:134; *Journal* for 7 November 1739, *Works* 19:120; letter to Miss Bishop (12 June 1773), Jackson 13:24; and letter to Hester Roe (11 February 1777), Jackson 13:79.

93. Letter to Miss Cooke (31 March 1787), Jackson 13:98; letter to Miss J. C. M. (3 June 1774), Jackson 13:50; letter to Miss J. C. M. (24 June 1764), Jackson 13:49; letter to Miss March (24 June 1764), Telford 4:251 and 270;

letter to Peggy Dale (8 February 1766), Telford 4:321; letter to Jane Hilton (22 July 1766), Telford 5:24; letter to Miss March (14 April 1771), Telford 5:238; letter to Ann Bolton (15 April 1771), Telford 5:238; and letter to Mary Stokes (January 1772), Telford 5:302. For a further discussion of these cautions, see Matthews, 173-80 and Jones, 71–73.

94. Letter to Miss J. C. M. (3 June 1774), Jackson 13:50.

95. Wesley's cautions often came personal letters of spiritual counsel to women. This is not surprising, given Wesley's apparent belief that a woman "is more easily deceived and more easily deceives"; her reason is more easily led astray. See Wesley's comments on 1 Timothy 2:14. *Explanatory Notes Upon the New Testament* (London: Epworth Press, 1952), 776. Matthews (176–77) suggests that Wesley's cautions stemmed not so much from sexism as from a pastoral concern. His cautions were designed to encourage someone who had expressed doubt to simply trust in God.

96. "The Case of Reason Impartially Considered," §§IV.1–3, *Works* 2:584–86.

97. See the discussion of Richard Hooker and his use of "reason" and "law," pp. 34–37 above.

Notes to Chapter Five

1. Letter to the editor, by Dolores Klinsky Walker, *United Methodist Reporter*, 143/11 (2 August 1996): 2.

2. My survey is informed by the article on "Experience" in *The Oxford English Dictionary*, rev. ed. (Oxford: Clarendon Press, 1989), 5:563–64; P. L. Heath, "Experience," in *The Encyclopedia of Philosophy*, ed. Paul Edwards (New York: Macmillan, 1967), 3:156–58; and James Alfred Martin, Jr., "Religious Experience," in *The Encyclopedia of Religion*, ed. Mircea Eliade (New York: Macmillan, 1987), 12:323–30.

3. *A Farther Appeal to Men of Reason and Religion*, Part II, §III.9, *Works* 11:258.

4. See definition 4b.

5. Letter to Dr. Henry Stebbing (25 July 1739), §6, *Works* 25:671.

6. *The Christian's Pattern; or, a Treatise of the Imitation of Christ*, Preface, §III.6, Jackson 14:207–8.

7. See respectively "On Visiting the Sick," §II.3, *Works* 3:390; and *Journal* for 5 June 1772, *Works* 22:336.

8. See how often he adds this comment in *Notes*: Matthew 16:21, Matthew 23:34, John 17:13, Acts 22:19, Romans 15:14, and Titus 2:3. But note as well his recognition that experience and age do not always go together, in letter to Miss March (27 December 1774), Telford 6:132.

9. *Journal* for 14 October 1769, *Works* 22:207.

10. Cited in definition 1a in the *Oxford English Dictionary*.

11. While Wesley did not include a definition of "experience" in *The*

Complete English Dictionary, 3rd ed. (London: Hawes, 1777), note that his definition for the closely related word "experiment" was "a proof, trial."

12. See *Primitive Physick*, Preface, §9, Jackson 14:310.

13. Ibid., §§4–7, Jackson 14:308–10.

14. *Journal* for 28 August 1736, *Works* 18:171.

15. *Journal* for 27 February 1740, *Works* 19:158.

16. The best account of this project, focused on René Descartes, is Stephen Toulmin, *Cosmopolis: The Hidden Agenda of Modernity* (New York: Free Press, 1990).

17. Cf. the discussion of epistemology in Randy L. Maddox, *Responsible Grace: John Wesley's Practical Theology* (Nashville: Kingswood Books, 1994), 27–28.

18. *A Letter to the Author of "The Enthusiasm of Methodists and Papists Compared,"* §32, *Works* 11:374. See also *The Doctrine of Original Sin*, Part IV, Essay I, §II, Jackson 9:386; where Wesley argues that claiming this life provides true happiness is "contrary to the common sense and experience of every thinking man."

19. "The First-fruits of the Spirit," §II.5, *Works* 1:239.

20. See *Journal* for 6 September 1742, *Works* 19:296; where Wesley interviews several persons who had testified about "feeling" the Spirit's work. He affirms their claim in relation to feeling the work of the Spirit of God in bestowing peace and joy and love. But he was much more skeptical of such things as feeling the blood of Christ running down their arms.

21. These debates are often framed in the language of coming to terms with our "post-modern" cultural situation. A good introduction to the issues involved is Walter Truett Anderson, ed., *The Truth about the Truth: De-Confusing and Re-Constructing the Postmodern World* (New York: G. P. Putnam's Sons, 1995).

22. *The Doctrine of Original Sin*, §II.13, Jackson 9:176.

23. "Original Sin," *Works* 2:172–85, esp. §II.2, 176.

24. See the discussion of these moves in Richard P. Heitzenrater, *Mirror and Memory: Reflections on Early Methodism* (Nashville: Kingswood Books, 1989), 106–49; and Maddox, *Responsible Grace*, 124–27.

25. Relate this to Wesley's concession already in 1750 that we cannot be sure that "invincible ignorance" (our prejudices) does not influence all of our beliefs; in "Catholic Spirit," §I.5, *Works* 2:84.

26. See Hume's *Treatise of Human Nature*, I.4.7; cf. Wesley, "The Deceitfulness of the Human Heart," §II.7, *Works* 4:158.

27. See "The Witness of the Spirit, II," §V.2, *Works* 1:297.

28. Letter to Mary Bishop (19 September 1773), Telford 6:44.

29. See letter to Mrs. Ryan (28 June 1766), Telford 5:16: "You appear to undervalue the experience of almost everyone in comparison of your own."

30. See his insistence that there is no holiness but social (i.e., com-

munal) holiness in *Hymns and Sacred Poems*, Preface §§4–5, Jackson 14:321; and "Sermon on the Mount, IV," §I.1, *Works* 1:533–34. On the role of conference in deciding doctrine, note the agenda for Wesley's conferences with his preachers set out in the Minutes of the very first meeting (25 June 1744), Jackson 8:275.

31. E.g., "The Character of a Methodist," §13, *Works* 9:39; "The Witness of the Spirit, I," §I.8, *Works* 1:274; "Sermon on the Mount, IV," §III.2, *Works* 1:542; and "The Unity of the Divine Being," §17, *Works* 4:67.

32. For more on Wesley's moral psychology, see Randy L. Maddox, "Holiness of Heart and Life: Lessons from North American Methodism," *Asbury Theological Journal* 51/1 (1996): 151–72.

33. Cf. "The Witness of the Spirit, I," *Works* 1:269–84; "The Witness of the Spirit, II," *Works* 1:285–98; and "The New Birth," §IV.4, *Works* 2:201.

34. "The Great Privilege of Those that are Born of God," §I.1–10, *Works* 1:432–34; "The New Birth," §II.4, *Works* 2:192; and "On Living Without God," *Works* 4:169–76.

35. Note how he equates the witness of the Spirit with "inward feeling" in *A Second Letter to the Author of "The Enthusiasm of Methodists and Papists Compared,"* §20, *Works* 11:399; and "Witness of the Spirit, II," §II.6, *Works* 1:288.

36. For a handy summary of this material, see Jeffrey Chamberlain, "Moralism, Justification, and the Controversy over Methodism," *Journal of Ecclesiastical History* 44 (1993): 652–78, esp. 668–70.

37. Cf. Maddox, *Responsible Grace*, 130.

38. See the discussion of the perceptibility of grace in Maddox, *Responsible Grace*, 128–29. The charges against Wesley are evident throughout the appeals gathered in Volume 11 of his *Works*. The debate was clouded by the failure of some of Wesley's opponents to recognize that he was using "inspiration" in a traditional sense of "animating or exciting"(cf. ibid., 121–22). One of his major qualifications is that while we experience the fruits of the Spirit's inspiration inwardly, we must turn to the Bible to determine whence they come; see his letter to Dr. Thomas Rutherforth (28 March 1768), §III.1, *Works* 9:381.

39. The most significant defense of Wesley's basic notion (without reference to him per se) is in William Alston, *Perceiving God* (Ithaca, NY: Cornell University Press, 1991), esp. 250. For an example of how this notion might be appropriated in our post-Enlightenment setting, see William J. Abraham, "The Epistemological Significance of the Inner Witness of the Holy Spirit," *Faith and Philosophy* 7 (1990): 434–50, esp. 447–48; and Maddox, *Responsible Grace*, 131.

40. See his letter to Thomas Maxfield reproduced in *Journal* for 29 October 1762, *Works* 21:396; and "The Nature of Enthusiasm," *Works* 2:46–60.

41. See especially letter to Dorothy Furly (21 October 1757), Telford 3:230; and letter to Mary Cooke (30 October 1785), Telford 7:298.

42. On Wesley's interest in the spiritual exemplars of the Early Church, see Ted A. Campbell, *John Wesley and Christian Antiquity: Religious Vision and Cultural Change* (Nashville: Kingswood Books, 1991), 55–71. Then note his appreciation of what some older members of the Methodist societies have learned by "dear-bought experience" in "On Visiting the Sick," §III.5, *Works* 3:394.

43. "The Scripture Way of Salvation," §I.7, *Works* 2:159. I emphasized "unexperienced" because it was inserted by Wesley to explain the term "unskillful" in Macarius's text (cf. *Wesley's Christian Library* [1749] 1:97).

44. I think of works like Roberta C. Bondi, *Memories of God: Theological Reflections on a Life* (Nashville: Abingdon Press, 1995), 7–11.

45. The most complete edition is the corrected 4th ed., 5 vols. (London: Maxwell & Wilson, 1809). For more on Wesley's empirical apologetic for God and debates about it, see Maddox, *Responsible Grace*, 34–35 (including notes).

46. On depravity, see *Doctrine of Original Sin*, Part II, §II.20, Jackson 9:295; Part III, §II, Jackson 9:318; Part III, §VII, Jackson 9:338; Part IV, Q. 1, §3, Jackson 9:361; and "Original Sin," §II.2, *Works* 2:176. On human liberty, see "What is Man?" §11, *Works* 4:24.

47. Perhaps the best example is in *A Letter to the Reverend Dr. Conyers Middleton*, §§II.12–III.12, Telford 2:383–87. See Maddox, *Responsible Grace*, 32.

48. See letter to Samuel Furly (21 May 1762), Telford 4:181; and "The Case of Reason Impartially Considered," §II.1–2, *Works* 2:593–94.

49. See the discussion of Wesley's anthropology, including the role of prevenient grace, in Maddox, *Responsible Grace*, 65–93.

50. Cf. his affirmation, "The World around us is a mighty volume wherein God hath declared himself," in *Survey* 2:125.

51. "Sermon on the Mount, I," §I.3, *Works* 1:476.

52. Note his formal defense of using experience to confirm Scripture in "The Witness of the Spirit, II," §V.2, *Works* 1:297.

53. E.g., letter to Charles Wesley (31 July 1747), *Works* 26:255; and "On Sin in Believers," §III.7, *Works* 1:323. Note that in both cases he argues that his opponent's position was contrary to Scripture as well as to experience. In reality, experience had helped him decide the most adequate understanding of Scripture on both issues.

54. *A Plain Account of the People Called Methodists*, §VI.7, *Works* 9:269.

55. See "On Patience," §§11–12, *Works* 3:177–78. Cf. his letter to Ann Loxdale (12 July 1782), Telford 7:129, where he refers to experience as "the strongest of all arguments." One must qualify this by remembering that he was dealing with a case on which he believed that Scripture was silent.

56. See Randy L. Maddox, "Opinion, Religion and 'Catholic Spirit': John Wesley on Theological Integrity," *Asbury Theological Journal* 47 (1992): 63–87, esp. 75–76.

57. See *A Second Letter to the Author of "The Enthusiasm of Methodists and Papists Compared,"* §20, *Works* 11:399; and *A Letter to the Right Reverend the Lord Bishop of London*, §6, *Works* 11:337. Note as well his response to reliance on the "Inner Light," in "Letter to a Person Lately Joined with the People Called Quakers" (10 February 1748), Telford 2:116–17.

58. See esp. "Witness of the Spirit, II," §III.6, *Works* 1:290.

59. Cf. *Thoughts on Christian Perfection*, Qq. 37–38, in Albert C. Outler, ed., *John Wesley* (New York: Oxford University Press, 1964), 297–98; letter to Mrs. Ryan (28 June 1766), Telford 5:16; letter to Charles Wesley (9 July 1766), Telford 5:20; letter to Charles Wesley (12 February 1767), Telford 5:41; and letter to Miss March (30 November 1774), Telford 6:129. Cf. the letter to John from Charles Wesley (28 February 1741), *Works* 26:52.

60. "Reasons Against a Separation from the Church of England," §III.2, *Works* 9:339–40. Cf. "Predestination Calmly Considered," §86, Jackson 10:256; and "Free Grace," *Works* 3:544–59.

61. Cf. his response to the appeal to experience by the quietists in "Sermon on the Mount, IV," §III.6, *Works* 1:545.

62. Preface to first volume of *Sermons*, §5, *Works* 1:105–6.

63. See the discussion of this in Hans-Georg Gadamer, *Truth and Method*, rev. ed. (New York: Crossroad, 1992), 265ff.

64. This story is told well in Paul W. Chilcote, *She Offered Them Christ: The Legacy of Women Preachers in Early Methodism* (Nashville: Abingdon Press, 1993).

65. *Doctrine of Original Sin*, Part I, §II.11, Jackson 9:228. See also Theodore W. Jennings, Jr., *Good News to the Poor: John Wesley's Evangelical Economics* (Nashville: Abingdon Press, 1990), esp. 47–69; and Pamela D. Couture, *Blessed Are the Poor? Women's Poverty, Family Policy, and Practical Theology* (Nashville: Abingdon Press, 1991), 119–34.

66. These examples of Wesley actually being benefited by conference need to be balanced against his clear self-image that he came to his conferences with his preachers to dispense "light" (i.e., insight) while all he expected to derive from them was "heat" (i.e., motivational encouragement); cf. *Journal* for 16 February 1760, *Works* 21:240.

67. For more on these points, see Randy L. Maddox, "Recovering Theology as a Practical Discipline: A Contemporary Agenda," *Theological Studies* 51 (1990): 650–72; and Maddox, "John Wesley—Practical Theologian?" *Wesleyan Theological Journal* 23 (1988): 122–47.

68. Note in this regard how he can admit that even the Anglican articles and homilies are products of fallible authors, yet insist that they are still *more* worthy of affirmation than most human compositions, in "Ought We to Separate from the Church of England?" §II.2, *Works* 9:569.

69. The reader may want to compare these suggestions to two recent (opposing) contributions to the present debate: John B. Cobb, Jr., *Grace and Responsibility: A Wesleyan Theology for Today* (Nashville: Abingdon Press, 1995), 159–76; and William J. Abraham, *Waking from Doctrinal*

Amnesia: The Healing of Doctrine in The United Methodist Church (Nashville: Abingdon Press, 1995), 61–63. Note as well how Wesley's model meets some of the concerns expressed in Owen C. Thomas, "Theology and Experience," *Harvard Theological Review* 78 (1985): 179–201. Most of Wesley's points find some mention in ¶68 of the United Methodist *Book of Discipline*, but they are presented in such "grab-bag" fashion that they have had little constructive impact on the debate.

70. See in this regard, Monika Hellwig, *Whose Experience Counts in Theological Reflection?* (Milwaukee, WI: Marquette University Press, 1982).

Note to Conclusion

1. The reader has perhaps noticed that in the body of our text we have usually listed and written about the Quadrilateral's components placing "experience" last, for as an addition to the formal categories "experience" came last in historical chronology. The exceptions to this are the specific references to *The Book of Discipline of The United Methodist Church*, in which "experience" precedes "reason."

Select Bibliography

Abraham, William J. "The Epistemological Significance of the Inner Witness of the Holy Spirit." *Faith and Philosophy* 7 (1990): 434–50.

———. *Waking from Doctrinal Amnesia: The Healing of Doctrine in The United Methodist Church*. Nashville: Abingdon Press, 1995.

Alston, William. *Perceiving God*. Ithaca, NY: Cornell University Press, 1991.

Ames, William. *The Marrow of Theology: William Ames, 1576-1633*. Edited and translated by John D. Eusden. Boston: Pilgrim Press, 1968.

Anderson, Walter Truett. *The Truth about the Truth: De-Confusing and Re-Constructing the Postmodern World*. New York: G. P. Putnam's Sons, 1995.

Andrewes, Lancelot. *Opuscula quaedam posthumata*. Oxford: John Henry Parker, 1852. Library of Anglo-Catholic Theology Edition.

Baker, Frank. "John Wesley and Bishop Joseph Butler: A Fragment of John Wesley's Manuscript Journal, 16th to 14th August 1793." *Proceedings of the Wesley Historical Society* 42 (May 1980): 97.

———. *John Wesley and the Church of England*. Nashville: Abingdon Press, 1970.

Becon, Thomas. *Prayers and Other Pieces of Thomas Becon*. Edited by Reverend John Ayre. Cambridge: Cambridge University Press, 1844.

Beveridge, William. ΣΥΝΟΔΙΚΟΝ, *sive Pandectae Canonum Ss. Apostolorum et Conciliorum Ecclesia graeca receptorum*. 2 vols. Oxford: William Wells and Robert Scott, 1672.

———. *Codex Canonum Ecclesiae primitivae vindicatus ac illustratus*. 2 vols. Oxford: John Henry Parker, 1847.

Bicknell, E. J. *A Theological Introduction to the Thirty-nine Articles*. London: Longmans, Green and Co., 1944 (1st ed., 1925).

Bondi, Roberta C. *Memories of God: Theological Reflections on a Life*. Nashville: Abingdon Press, 1995.

The Book of Discipline of The United Methodist Church, 1996. Nashville: The United Methodist Publishing House, 1996.

Booty, John E., editor. *John Jewel as Apologist of the Church of England*. London: SPCK, 1963.

Brantley, Richard E. *Locke, Wesley, and the Method of English Romanticism*. Gainesville, FL: University of Florida Press, 1984.

Bull, George. *Defensio Fidei Nicaenae: A Defense of the Nicene Creed, out of the Extant Writings of the Catholick Doctors, who Flourished during the First Three Centuries of the Christian Church*. 2 vols. Oxford: John Henry Parker, 1851.

——. *The Judgment of the Catholic Church on the Necessity of Believing that our Lord Jesus Christ is Very God*. Oxford: John Henry Parker, 1855.

Campbell, Ted A. *Christian Confessions: A Historical Introduction*. Louisville: Westminster/John Knox Press, 1996.

——. "Christian Tradition, John Wesley, and Evangelicalism." *Anglican Theological Review* 74/1 (winter 1992): 54–67.

——. "Is It Just Nostalgia? The Renewal of Wesleyan Studies." *Christian Century* 107/13 (18 April 1990): 398–98.

——. *John Wesley and Christian Antiquity: Religious Vision and Cultural Change*. Nashville: Kingswood Books, 1991.

——. "John Wesley's Conceptions and Uses of Christian Antiquity." Ph.D. diss., Southern Methodist University, 1984.

——. "The 'Wesleyan Quadrilateral': The Story of a Modern Methodist Myth." In *Doctrine and Theology in The United Methodist Church*, edited by Thomas A. Langford, 154-61. Nashville: Kingswood Books, 1991.

Cave, William. *Primitive Christianity: or, the Religion of the Ancient Christians in the First Ages of the Gospel*. London: Thomas Tegg, 1840.

Cell, George C. *The Rediscovery of John Wesley*. New York: Henry Holt, 1935.

Chamberlain, Jeff. "Moralism, Justification, and the Controversy over Methodism." *Journal of Ecclesiastical History* 44 (1993): 652–78.

Chilcote, Paul W. *She Offered Them Christ: The Legacy of Women Preachers in Early Methodism*. Nashville: Abingdon Press, 1993.

Chiles, Robert E. *Theological Transition in American Methodism: 1790–1935*. Reprint. Lanham, MD: University Press of America, 1983.

Cobb, Jr., John B. *Grace and Responsibility: A Wesleyan Theology for Today*. Nashville: Abingdon Press, 1995.

The Concise Oxford English Dictionary. Oxford: Oxford University Press, 1976.

Corrie, G. E., editor. *The Sermons and Remains of Hugh Latimer*. 2 vols. Cambridge: Cambridge University Press, 1844-45.

Couture, Pamela D. *Blessed Are the Poor? Women's Poverty, Family Policy, and Practical Theology*. Nashville: Abingdon Press, 1991.

Cragg, Gerald R. *Freedom and Authority: A Study of English Thought in the Early Seventeenth Century*. Philadelphia: The Westminster Press, 1975.

——. *Reason and Authority in the Eighteenth Century*. Cambridge: Cambridge University Press, 1964.

Cranmer, Thomas. *The Remains of Thomas Cranmer*. Edited by H. Jenkyns. 4 vols. Oxford: Oxford University Press, 1833.

Curnock, Nehemiah, editor. *The Journal of the Rev. John Wesley, A.M.* 8 vols. London: Epworth Press, 1909–1916, repr. in 1938.

Daillé, John [Jean]. *A Treatise concerning the Right Use of the Fathers*. Translated by Thomas Smith. London: John Martin, 1651.

Davies, Horton. *Worship and Theology in England*, Vol. 1: *From Cranmer to Hooker, 1534–1603*. Princeton: Princeton University Press, 1970.

Deacon, Thomas. *Compleat Collection of Devotions*. London: printed for the author, 1734.

English, John C. "The Cambridge Platonists in John Wesley's Christian Library." *Proceedings of the Wesley Historical Society* 37 (1970): 101–4.

Frere, W. H. and C. E. Douglas, editors. *Puritan Manifestoes; A Study of the Origin of the Puritan Revolt*. With a reprint of the *Admonition to the Parliament*. 2nd ed. London: SPCK, 1954.

——. *The English Church in the Reigns of Elizabeth and James I (1558-1625)*. London and New York: Macmillan, 1904.

——, and W. M. Kennedy. *Visitation Articles and Injunctions. Period of the Reformation*. 3 vols. New York: Longmans, Green and Co., 1910.

"A Fruitful Exhortation to the Reading of the Holy Scripture." In *Certain Sermons or Homilies Appointed to be Read in Churches in the Time of Queen Elizabeth of Famous Memory*. London: SPCK, 1890.

Gadamer, Hans-Georg. *Truth and Method*. Rev. ed. New York: Crossroad, 1992.

Gay, Peter. *The Enlightenment: An Interpretation*, Vol. 1: *The Rise of Modern Paganism*. New York and London: The W. W. Norton Co., 1966.

Gee, H., and W. J. Hardy, editors. *Documents Illustrative of English Church History*. London: Macmillan, 1921 (1st ed. 1896).

The Great Bible. A Facsimile of the 1539 Edition. Tokyo: Elpis,Co., Ltd., 1991.

Greenslade, Stanley Lawrence. *The English Reformers and the Fathers of the Church*. Oxford: Clarendon Press, 1960.

Grindal, Edmund. *The Remains of [Archbishop]Edmund Grindal, Successively Bishop of London and Archbishop of York and Canterbury*. Edited by W. Nicholson. Cambridge: Cambridge University Press, 1843.

Gunter, W. Stephen. *The Limits of 'Love Divine': John Wesley's Response to Antinomianism and Enthusiasm*. Nashville: Kingswood Books, 1989.

Heath, P. L. "Experience." In *Encyclopedia of Philosophy* 3:156–58. Edited by Paul Edwards. New York: Macmillan, 1967.

Hellwig, Monika. *Whose Experience Counts in Theological Reflection?* Milwaukee, WI: Marquette University Press, 1982.

Heitzenrater, Richard P. *The Elusive Mr. Wesley: John Wesley as Seen by Contemporaries and Biographers*. 2 vols. Nashville: Abingdon Press, 1984.

——. *Mirror and Memory: Reflections on Early Methodism*. Nashville: Kingswood Books, 1989.

——. *Wesley and the People Called Methodists*. Nashville: Abingdon Press, 1995.

Hodges, J. P. *The Nature of the Lion: Elizabeth I and Our Anglican Heritage*. London: Faith Press, 1962.

Hooker, Richard. *Of the Laws of Ecclesiastical Polity*. Vol. 5 in *The Folger Library Edition of the Works of Richard Hooker*, edited by Georges Edelin et al. Cambridge, MA: The Belknap Press of Harvard University Press, 1977.

——. *The Works of Mr. Richard Hooker*. 3 vols. Edited by John Keble. Oxford: University Press, 1888.

Jackson, Thomas, editor. *The Works of the Reverend John Wesley, M.A.* 3rd ed. 14 vols. London: Wesleyan Methodist Book Room, 1872; many reprints.

Jennings, Theodore W., Jr. *Good News to the Poor: John Wesley's Evangelical Economics*. Nashville: Abingdon Press, 1990.

Jewel, John. *An Apology of the Church of England*. Edited by J. E. Booty. Ithaca, NY: Cornell University Press for the Folger Shakespeare Library, 1963.

——. *The Works of John Jewel*. 8 vols. Edited by Richard W. Jelf. Oxford: University Press, 1848.

Jones, Scott J. *John Wesley's Conception and Use of Scripture*. Nashville: Kingswood Books, 1995.

Kelsey, David. *The Uses of Scripture in Recent Theology*. Philadelphia: Fortress, 1975.

King, Peter. *An Enquiry into the Constitution, Discipline, Unity, and Worship of the Primitive Church*. New York: P. P. Sandford, 1841.

Langford, Thomas A., editor. *Doctrine and Theology in The United Methodist Church*. Nashville: Kingswood Books, 1991.

Lathbury, Thomas. *A History of the Non-Jurors*. London: William Pickering, 1845.

Latimer, Hugh. *The Sermons of Bishop Latimer*. Edited by G. E. Corrie. Cambridge: Cambridge University Press, 1844-45.

——. *Sermons and Remains of Hugh Latimer*. Edited by G. E. Corrie. Cambridge: University Press, 1845.

Leupp, Roderick T. "'The Art of God': Light and Darkness in the Thought of John Wesley." Ph.D. diss., Drew University, 1985.

Link, Hans-Georg, editor. *Apostolic Faith Today: A Handbook for Study*. Faith and Order Paper no. 124. Geneva: World Council of Churches, 1985.

Luoma, John K. "Who Owns the Fathers? Hooker and Cartwright on the Authority of the Primitive Church," *Sixteenth Century Journal* 8 (1977): 53–58.

Maddox, Randy L. "Holiness of Heart and Life: Lessons from North American Methodism." *Asbury Theological Journal* 51/1 (1996): 151–72.

——. "John Wesley—Practical Theologian?" *Wesleyan Theological Journal* 23 (1988): 122–47.

——. "Opinion, Religion and 'Catholic Spirit': John Wesley on Theological Integrity." *Asbury Theological Journal* 47 (1992): 63–87.

——. "Recovering Theology as a Practical Discipline: A Contemporary Agenda." *Theological Studies* 51 (1990): 650–72.

——. *Responsible Grace: John Wesley's Practical Theology*. Nashville: Kingswood Books, 1994.

Martin, James A., Jr. "Religious Experience." In *The Encyclopedia of Religion*, edited by Mircea Eliade, vol. 12: 323–30. New York: Macmillan, 1987.

Marshall, Nathaniel. *The Penitential Discipline of the Primitive Church*. Oxford: John Henry Parker, 1844.

Matthews, Rex D. "'Religion and Reason Joined': A Study in the Theology of John Wesley." Th.D. diss., Harvard University, 1986.

McAdoo, Henry R. "Richard Hooker." In *The English Religious Tradition and the Genius of Anglicanism*, edited by Geoffrey Rowell, 105–25. Nashville: Abingdon Press, 1992.

——. *The Spirit of Anglicanism: A Survey of Anglican Theological Methodology in the Seventeenth Century*. New York: Charles Scribner's Sons, 1965.

———. *The Structure of Caroline Moral Theology*. London: Longmans, Green, and Co., 1949.

———. *The Unity of Anglicanism: Catholic and Reformed*. Wilton, CT: Morehouse, 1983.

Moorman, John R. H. *A History of the Church in England*. New York: Morehouse Barlow, 1973 (1st edition, 1953)

Outler, Albert C. "A New Future for Wesley Studies: An Agenda for 'Phase III.'" In *The Future of the Methodist Theological Traditions*, edited by M. Douglas Meeks, 34–52. Nashville: Abingdon Press, 1985.

———. "The Wesleyan Quadrilateral—in John Wesley." In *Doctrine and Theology in The United Methodist Church*, edited by Thomas A. Langford, 75–88. Nashville: Kingswood Books, 1991.

———, editor. *John Wesley*. A Library of Protestant Thought. New York: Oxford University Press, 1964.

———, and Richard P. Heitzenrater, editors. *John Wesley's Sermons: An Anthology*. Nashville: Abingdon Press, 1991.

The Oxford English Dictionary. Rev. ed. Prepared by J. A. Simpson and E. S. C. Weiner. Oxford: Clarendon Press, 1989. Article on "Experience." Vol. 5:563–64.

Parrott, Bob, editor. *Albert Outler: The Churchman*. Anderson, IN: Bristol House, 1995.

Pearson, A. F. Scott, *Thomas Cartwright and Elizabethan Puritanism*. Cambridge: Cambridge University Press, 1925.

Pearson, John. *Vindiciae Epistolarum S. Ignatii*. 2 vols. Oxford: John Henry Parker, 1852.

"Promise Keepers, UMC Can Learn From One Another," *The United Methodist Reporter* (8 November 1996).

Prothero, G. W., editor. *Select Statutes and Other Constitutional Documents*. Oxford: Clarendon Press, 1913.

Proudfoot, Wayne. *Religious Experience*. Berkeley, CA: University of California Press, 1985.

Schmidt, Martin. *John Wesley: A Theological Biography*. 2 vols. in 3. Translated by Norman Goldhawk and Denis Inman. Nashville: Abingdon Press, 1963–73.

Shimizu, Mitsuo. "Epistemology in the Thought of John Wesley." Ph.D. diss., Drew University, 1980.

Stillingfleet, Edward. *The Irenicum: or, Pacificator*. Philadelphia: M. Sorin, 1842.

Strype, John. *The Life and Acts of Matthew Parker*. London: Printed for John Wyatt, 1711.

———. *Ecclesiastical Memorials*. 3 vols. London: Printed for John Wyatt, 1721.

Tanner, Joseph R., editor. *Tudor Constitutional Documents, A.D. 1485–1603*. Cambridge: Cambridge University Press, 1930.

Telford, John, editor. *The Letters of The Rev. John Wesley, A.M.* 8 vols. London: Epworth Press, 1931.

Thomas, Owen C. "Theology and Experience." *Harvard Theological Review* (1985): 179–201.

Thorsen, Donald A. D. *The Wesleyan Quadrilateral: Scripture, Tradition, Reason and Experience as a Model of Evangelical Theology.* Grand Rapids, MI: Zondervan, 1990.

Toulmin, Stephen. *Cosmopolis: The Hidden Agenda of Modernity.* New York: Free Press, 1990.

Urlin, R. Denny. *Churchman's Life of Wesley.* Rev. ed. London: SPCK, 1880.

Walker, Dolores Klinsky. "Letter to the Editor." *United Methodist Reporter* 143/11 (2 August 1996): 2.

Wesley, Charles. *The Young Student's Library.* Attributed to Samuel as president of the Athenian Society. London: John Dutton, 1692.

——. *Advice to a Young Clergyman, in a Letter to Him.* London: C. Rivington, 1735.

Wesley, John. *Explanatory Notes Upon the New Testament.* London: Wesleyan-Methodist Book Room, n.d.

——. *The Letters of John Wesley.* 8 vols. Edited by John Telford. London: Epworth Press, 1931.

——. *The Sunday Service of the Methodists in North America.* London: 1784. Reprinted by *Quarterly Review*, 1984.

——. *A Survey of the Wisdom of God in the Creation; or, A Compendium of Natural Philosophy.* 2 vols. 1st ed. London: 1763.

——. *The Works of John Wesley.* Edited by Frank Baker and Richard P. Heitzenrater. Vols. 7, 11, 25 & 26: The Oxford Edition, Oxford: Clarendon Press, 1975–83. All other vols.: Bicentennial Edition, Nashville: Abingdon Press, 1984—.

——. *The Works of The Rev. John Wesley, M.A.* Edited by Thomas Jackson. 3rd ed. 14 vols. London: Wesleyan Methodist Book Room, 1872. Reprinted, Grand Rapids: Zondervan, 1958–59.

Whitgift, John. *Works.* Vol. 1: The *Defence of the Answer to the Admonition Against the Reply of T[homas] C[artwright].* Drawn from Cartwright's *Admonition.* Edited by J. Ayre. Cambridge: Cambridge University Press, 1851–53.

Williams, Colin W. *John Wesley's Theology Today.* New York and Nashville: Abingdon Press, 1960.

Williams, John. *A Catechism Truly Representing the Doctrines and Practices of the Church of Rome, with an Answer Thereunto.* London: n.p., 1686.

Wood, Lawrence W. "Wesley's Epistemology." *Wesleyan Theological Journal* 10 (1975): 48–59.

Contributors

W. Stephen Gunter was educated at Willem de Zwijger Lyceum, Southern Nazarene University, Nazarene Theological Seminary, and The University of Leiden, The Netherlands. He previously taught at the Europäische Nazarener Bibelschule und Seminar and at Southern Nazarene University, where he served sequential roles as Religion Department Chair and College Dean. Currently he is the Arthur J. Moore Associate Professor of Evangelism at The Candler School of Theology, Emory University. His published works include *The Limits of 'Love Divine'* (1989) and a translation of Manfred Marquardt, *John Wesley's Social Ethics* [*Praxis und Prinzipien der Sozialethik John Wesleys*] (1992). Stephen wrote chapter one, "The Quadrilateral and the 'Middle Way,'" and served as the editor and coordinator for this project.

Scott J. Jones was born to a Methodist parsonage and raised in Illinois, Indiana, and Colorado. He was educated at the University of Kansas, The Perkins School of Theology, and Southern Methodist University. He has served as pastor of United Methodist churches in Prosper, Howe, and Commerce, Texas, and is now the McCreless Assistant Professsor of Evangelism at Perkins School of Theology. Jones' publications include *John Wesley's Conception and Use of Scripture* (1995). Scott authored chapter two, "The Rule of Scripture."

Ted A. Campbell was educated at Lon Morris College, the University of North Texas, Oxford University, and Southern Methodist University. He has served as pastor of United Methodist congregations, and has taught at the Methodist Theological School in Ohio, Duke Divinity School, and Wesley Theological Seminary, where he currently serves as Professor of the History of Christianity. His published works include *John Wesley and Christian Antiquity* (1991), *The Religion of the Heart* (1991), and *Christian Confessions* (Westminster/John Knox Press, 1996). Ted authored chapter three, "The Interpretive Role of Tradition."

Rebekah L. Miles was educated at Hendrix College, The Iliff School of Theology, and the University of Chicago. She is currently Assistant Professor of Christian Ethics at Brite Divinity School, Texas Christian University, where she directs the United Methodist Studies Program. She and her husband, Len Delony, a hospital chaplain, are clergy members of the Little Rock Conference where they once served a rural two-point charge. Rebekah's publications include articles on Georgia Harkness and A. C. Knudson in *Makers of Christian Theology in America*, ed. Mark G. Toulouse and James O. Duke (1997), and *Moral Guides: A Practrical Guide to Ethics and Pastoral Care* (forthcoming, 1998). For this project she authored chapter four, "The Instrumental Role of Reason."

Randy L. Maddox was educated at Northwest Nazarene College, Nazarene Theological Seminary, and Emory University. He is currently Professor of Religion and Philosophy at the University of Sioux Falls, as well as adjunct professor of religion and professor of Methodist Studies at the North American Baptist Seminary. In addition to being past president of the Wesleyan Theological Society, Randy is presently co-chair of the Wesleyan Studies Group of the American Academy of Religion. In addition to numerous scholarly articles, Randy's publications include *Aldersgate Reconsidered* (1990) and *Responsible Grace: John Wesley's Practical Theology* (1994). He authored chapter five, "The Enriching Role of Experience."